The author is a full-time professional punter who makes a steady and lucrative income from gambling. In this book he reveals, for the first time, the techniques and methods that consistently give him the edge over bookmakers.

Any backer can improve their betting performance substantially by learning to bet like a professional. *Against The Crowd* gives this information and anyone who bets on horses will find valuable insights on how to become - and stay - a winner.

AGAINST THE CROWD

The methods of a modern backer

ALAN POTTS

Acknowledgements

With grateful thanks to Ian Carnaby for the support and encouragement that led to this book seeing the light of day.

And to Mark Coton and Nick Mordin whose earlier books provided the example which I have followed.

Cover design by Mouse House Print Shop, Hale, Cheshire

First Published 1995
by Aesculus Press,
P.O.Box 10, Oswestry,
Shropshire SY11 1RB.

First reprint June 1996
Second reprint February 1997
Third reprint June 1998

Fourth reprint February 1999 (Rowton Press Ltd)
Fifth reprint October 1999
Sixth reprint November 2000
Seventh reprint December 2003 (Aesculus Press Ltd)

Typeset by Aesculus Press using MICROSOFT WORD
Output on a Hewlett Packard HP Laserjet 4.

Printed and bound in Great Britain by
Ashford Colour Press Ltd, Gosport, Hampshire

1904328180

Preface

If the words 'professional gambler' summon up a picture of a sharp operator with a year-long suntan, expensive clothes, a page 3 bimbo in close attendance and a top of the range BMW in the car park, then I suggest you put this book back on the shelf and move on rapidly to the Romantic Fiction section.

If, on the other hand, they prompt ideas of a 'Robbie Box' type, as depicted in the TV series *Big Deal*, perpetually down to his last ten quid, ducking and diving from one shady deal to another, and surrounded by a bunch of friends who look as if they failed their auditions for *Eastenders* because they were either too scruffy or too miserable, then perhaps you should try looking in the Humour section.

There may well be people who fit the stereotypes described above, but they are conspicuous by their absence from the world I inhabit. It is precisely because of these predictable reactions that I personally dislike the term 'professional gambler'; but no widely understood alternative exists to describe someone whose sole income is obtained by betting.

This book describes how I came to be backing horses for a living, the methods I use and the experience I've gained from 30 years of involvement with racing.

I've no desire to convert readers into following my footsteps into what is, by necessity, a profession with a limited number of practitioners. But for those who enjoy betting on horses, on or off the racecourse, I hope it will provide some different insights into the game.

Contents

Introduction

I made my first bet on a horse race when I was about 13 years old. A school friend with an early beard and a Schwarzenegger build placed the bet for me in one of the new-fangled betting shops which had just been legalised. The stake was 2s 6d (12.5p) each way, the race a three-mile chase, and the horse, whose name I've long since forgotten, finished third at 6-1. In those halcyon days of one-quarter the odds each-way and no betting tax, I received a return of 6s 3d. Like so many before me, I was hooked.

I saw my first live horse race about two years later at the now sadly defunct Alexandra Park course, which was located only four or five miles from my home. Like most novices, I had no idea what was going on. The races were a blur, the results an enigma until announced over the loudspeaker, and betting with on-course bookmakers seemed as mysterious a ritual as anything offered up by Hammer horror at the local Odeon. But the air of excitement was tangible; the seedy nature of the surroundings highly attractive to a well scrubbed Grammar School boy. I was hooked all over again.

Long before I left school, my interest had led me to a part-time job as the Saturday boardboy in my local betting shop. Apart from the pleasures of working in the cramped space behind the counter with two women who seemed to be advanced suffragettes for the Swinging Sixties (the aroma of an old-fashioned felt tip pen can still induce erotic fantasies even after 30 years!), the customers introduced me to sections of society who would never have crossed my path elsewhere. But perhaps most importantly I learnt much about the many varieties of mug punter who keep such shops in business - lessons that took many years to learn, but which have stood me in good stead.

When I moved on to full-time employment, as a computer operator with IBM in the City of London, I soon identified the gamblers amongst my new colleagues. Many happy afternoons were spent in a huge cavern betting shop under a railway arch at Broad Street station, and many evenings (and nights) in friendly brag and poker sessions. And as I progressed through various jobs with computers during the late sixties and seventies, so I frequented a series of betting shops and race courses, mug punting with the rest of the crowd. I never read anything more advanced than *The Sporting Life*, and often that was only the copy on the betting shop wall - my only concession to any sort of sophistication was the purchase of the *Timeform Annual*, beginning with *Racehorses of 1970*.

Funds were a continual problem, despite a decent income and full employment. As with all mug punters there were successful spells, most of which I can still fondly recall, but mainly there was a steady trickle of losses which were soon forgotten. I always felt I had the capability of winning, if only I could bring some sort of control to the process, but I had no idea how to go about it. I knew I should keep records of my betting, and made several starts on such a process, but the recording would always stop as soon as I hit a losing run.

The key to changing my status from mug punter to serious punter came in 1978. I was working at a computer centre in Hounslow, which employed some temporary staff from a local agency. A consultant at the agency, who handled other business, was an ex-colleague from British Airways, and in June 1978 he was asked to find three experienced computer staff to go and work in Kuwait City at the government computer centre. I was approached, and as the job offered £1,000 per month tax free, it is fair to say that I practically bit off his hand.

I worked in Kuwait for two years, until the outbreak of the Iran/Iraq war (devout cowards live longer in my view). I was housed in a flat with the other two English staff, one of whom I had met before and who shared my passion for racing. He introduced me to the *Raceform Notebook*, which he'd arranged to have delivered to Kuwait, and I soon realised that one part of the jigsaw had fallen into place. And most importantly of all, at the end of our first year, in collaboration with a third expatriate we had met through playing poker, we arranged to become joint owners of a racehorse.

The full story of my experiences as an owner has no place in this book, but it transformed my outlook as a punter. Going racing with the trainer, I learnt to read a race; I learnt about all the things that can go wrong with these delicate creatures; I learnt about assessing the opposition; and perhaps most significantly, I learnt about the importance of placing your horse in a race that offers the right combination of distance, going and class on a day when he is fit and ready to perform. I discovered that newspapers would tip my horse on days when I knew it had little or no chance, and ignore it when I knew it had every chance. I discovered that a horse could start favourite, even though the owner could see quite clearly in the paddock that the horse wasn't fully fit. I discovered that after one bad run as second favourite, for which I knew the reason, the horse would start at generous odds next time against weaker opposition.

And crucially, I found that my two years away from day-to-day punting had enabled me to discover the essential control that meant I bet when it was right to do so, and not simply because I had time to go to a betting shop. Increasingly, I stopped using betting shops and concentrated my efforts on the race course, which I was visiting frequently as an owner.

My new job was based in Swindon, which it soon became obvious was an ideal base, with race courses accessible in all directions. The job required me to work flexible hours, the managers were happy to accommodate my half-days at the races, and a company car eliminated travelling expenses. From the date of my return from Kuwait in November 1980, I became a serious punter. I recorded all my bets, and retain those records to this day. I used a video recorder to enable me to watch meetings I couldn't attend. I subscribed to a weekly formbook for both Flat and National Hunt. I became an annual member at Cheltenham and Newbury, and I continued my career as an owner until the fund I'd accumulated in Kuwait for the purpose had been exhausted.

My staking levels remained relatively modest through the early and mid-eighties, but started to increase dramatically from 1988 onwards after the on-course tax was removed and, as I proved via my records, that I could consistently win money. In 1985, for example, my turnover was £20,000 and my profit of around £1,000 was almost entirely wiped out by the four per cent on-course tax. By 1991 that turnover figure had increased to £100,000, where it has remained each year since.

By 1991, I had often discussed with a close friend the idea of making a full-time living from punting, and planned to retire in my early fifties after I'd paid off my mortgage and acquired a few more years' experience with the protection of a good salary. Compulsory redundancy in November 1991 put an end to that plan, and within a few weeks I had decided that I would make the attempt now, rather than live to regret a missed opportunity later in life. Given that the employment opportunities for 40+ computer experts in 1991/2 resembled the stud prospects of a Bath selling race winner, the alternatives were pretty grim anyway!

The first year was heavy going as I adapted to the differing requirements of betting for the food money, rather than for fun. Had I been going to give up and slink off to the DHSS, then September 1992 would have offered the perfect opportunity. Having made a successful visit to the York Ebor meeting, where I netted a profit that put me £6,500 in front for the year, I embarked on a losing run that continued through to the end of September.

The run lasted five and a half weeks and contained 37 consecutive losers, which cost me £11,100. By the final day (Monday, September 28 at Bath), I had quite definitely reverted to my bad habits of the seventies, and my losses that day included £200 on a sprint handicap at Hamilton! The final bet, in the mile-and-a-half handicap at Bath, led two out but was headed in the final 50 yards. It finished second, as had eight of the preceding 36. One memorable loser had been beaten at 11-4 in a minor event at Salisbury, and had gone on to win a Group 2 contest at Doncaster at 33-1 just nine days later!

Following the Bath meeting, I stopped betting on the Flat for that season, and after a good deal of hard thinking, decided that I would continue through the coming NH season before making a final decision. My second bet over the jumps, two weeks later, was a 5-1 winner; and at the Ascot pre-Xmas meeting I collected £4,000 when Vagog won the Long Walk hurdle, a win that put my betting account for the calendar year just into the black, although insufficient to cover my expenses.

The final transformation came on the Friday after the 1993 Cheltenham Festival, when I spent five hours working on a Jackpot perm for the Lingfield meeting, which had the benefit of a £110,000 carry forward from Cheltenham. My £80 perm was successful and I collected £39,046 from Tote Credit. Apart from the boost to my capital, the injection of confidence I got from that win has been with me ever since and I can report steady profits on a regular basis.

But I remain aware this is difficult game, and that nobody is immune to losing runs or to loss of confidence. There are no fortunes to be made from full-time punting, but there is a steady income for the hard working and the competent. Although I now talk of going racing as going to work, I still love the atmosphere on the racecourse, and most of all I still love those marvellous, maddening, unpredictable but beautiful creatures that provide the sport. After all these years, I'm still hooked.

14 . Against The Crowd

Chapter One

The Four C's

This chapter defines my idea of the four essential qualities needed to be a successful punter. If parts of what follows strike you as unkind, even unpleasant, remember that the successful performers in most individual sports have a ruthless streak - and there is nothing more individual than backing horses.

Confidence

Anyone who has read accounts of successful gambles (real or mythical), or has perused the enticing adverts of the tipping services will be familiar with the oft-used cliche that the participants have 'bashed the bookies', or 'left the layers gasping'. The clear impression given is that, when you back a winner, the payout comes straight from the bookmakers' pocket.

Not to put too fine a point on it, this is a load of b*****ks! Examination of the published accounts for the big three chains of betting shops show annual profit figures which regularly exceed the total sum raised for racing via the Betting Levy. And, although on-course bookmakers have rivalled farmers in recent years in their tales of how badly things compare with the good old days, the same old faces are still present week in, week out, demonstrating the same old suntans and travelling in the same old gas guzzlers.

If you play a session of poker with friends, at the end of the evening it's obvious that the total amounts won by the successful players must equal the losses suffered by the others (the fact that this never seems to happen is a topic for discussion elsewhere!). On a racecourse the same logic applies, except that the bookies act as agents for the market and take a percentage of the losers' money before redistributing it among the winners. This may not happen after every race, but over a period of time the analogy holds good.

The crux is that winning punters do not take their profits from the bookies, but from losing punters. If we envisage a racecourse crowd of ten thousand souls on a Saturday, who produce an average stake of £50 per head over the day, then we have a total turnover of half a million pounds. If we assume 80 per cent of that will be returned as winnings (so Mr Average loses ten pounds on the day), and five per cent is used to cover the expenses of the bookies, betting shops and Tote, then £75,000 is left as profit for those agencies. All I am trying to do is to extract a small piece of that sum before it reaches its natural home.

To achieve this objective I need losing punters, just as surely as the bookies do. The figures above are guess-work, but they adequately demonstrate the principles. Every time I leave the racecourse at the end of a day's work, with a profit tucked into my zipped pocket, I offer a silent thank you to the mugs who make it possible - my fellow punters. Overall I regard the rest of the crowd with contempt, and use the term 'mug punter' as a collective noun in much the same dismissive way that I might say 'Arsenal supporters'. In neither case is this anything personal - I have friends who are mug punters and even friends who are Arsenal supporters - it is simply that one is a necessary part of my chosen occupation, and the other results from being a member of a North London family of lifelong Spurs fans.

Faced with my imaginary crowd of 10,000, I expect to win, because I am confident I know more than they do about racing, confident I know more than they do about betting, and confident I can use my knowledge to extract a profit from their ignorance.

Faced with a losing run, I am confident that if I continue to apply my methods consistently and stick to my rules, things will eventually turn in my favour.

In the midst of a winning run, I am confident I can take maximum advantage and generate maximum revenue from my successes.

Confronted by a Saturday in mid-summer with 30 or more races available, I'm confident I can identify those that provide me with the best opportunities.

If this sounds suspiciously like arrogance, then I have to agree. But who is going to read a book in which the first chapter is titled 'One A and Three Cs'?

Capital

If you seriously want to make a living from betting, you need a sizeable capital bank before you start. In my view the amount required can be calculated as being a minimum of five times the annual profit you hope to generate. Apart from acting as a safety net in bad times, this capital can generate an income via investment, which will help to offset your racing expenses.

I recognise that for most people this is an impossible figure, but consideration of the reasoning behind it appears later in the chapter on money management.

At a fun, but serious betting level, I strongly recommend building up a separate capital base - i.e. keep the money in a separate account, keep the cash in a separate wallet, one you use on racedays. With proper discipline, this avoids the danger of betting the mortgage money when a 'good thing' looms in the last race after a bad day.

Your cheque book and/or credit card should never accompany you to a betting shop or a racecourse!

Calculation

In the betting ring immediately before a race, things happen very quickly. The two most important decisions involved in placing a bet are:

'How much am I going to stake?'
'What is the price I'm going to take?'

Much more on these questions later in the chapters covering the betting market and money management, but both require speed of thought under pressure, and the quicker you can do the necessary calculations the better. Don't take the view that you can't learn how to do it because you're 'No good with figures'.

Most darts players can't add up 161 and 180 in their heads, but they can subtract the same figures from 501 without even knowing how they do it. The same applies to betting - it's a small specialisation that anyone can grasp with practice.

Cynicism

By far the most important of the four C's. John McCririck has often warned C4 viewers that the time to beware is when all the racing hacks agree - he is dead right. As far as the topic of this book is concerned, the vast majority of the people professionally involved in racing, such as jockeys, trainers and journalists, are a complete waste of space.

The opinions of jockeys and trainers can be dismissed immediately as the inevitably biased reports of those who are closely involved with one horse in a race. What they know about the other contestants, they probably got from the journalists.

There are a few exceptions, such as Martin Pipe, who employ the services of form analysts to check out the opposition. But speaking as someone who has owned horses, I reckon most trainers fail even to spot the obvious clues about their own horses as to their going, distance and course preferences. When jockeys are interviewed, any quotes they offer should be reviewed with the point firmly in mind that the number one objective is to keep their rides and their jobs.

Think of the number of times you've heard a jockey say that the horse he has just ridden is the best he has ever sat on, or words to that effect. And think of the number of times a stable jockey, given a choice of two runners in the same big race, picks the wrong one, and remember he is probably following the advice of the trainer.

As for the regular racing journalists, it's probable that the only equivalent gatherings of smug, self-satisfied somnolent sheep exist inside the offices of the MCC and the Rugby Union. With a few honourable exceptions, their entire existence revolves around the winners' enclosure and the press room, wherein they can reinforce each other's good opinion of themselves. Since the number of journalists who actually come and look at the horses in the parade ring, place a cash bet with a Tatts bookie, or watch races from somewhere where they might see the guts of the action rather than on the press room TV, can be counted on the fingers of a convicted Iraqi pickpocket, we can ignore their views entirely when it comes to analysing a race.

So there we have the four C's - Confidence, Capital, Calculation and Cynicism. Four essential weapons in the armoury of a successful backer. Form your own opinions and take those of others with a large pinch of salt, decide how to act on the results of your analysis, with the resources available, and above all, have confidence in your ultimate success.

The Four C's in practice

At various points in this book, I'll use examples from my own recent experiences to demonstrate the points made in the particular chapter. Most, but not all, of these pieces will be about winners, but the reader should always remind himself that for every winner, there are multiple losers.

Confidence can run thin during a long losing run. By the close of play on November 11, 1993, my record for the NH season thus far contained just three winners at short prices and 18 losers. The net loss was over £5,000. Friday, November 12 was the start of the Mackeson meeting at Cheltenham - feature race the eight-runner Young Chasers Final Handicap over three-miles, one-furlong. Two of the runners had featured in my list of 40 horses to follow, prepared in September as follows:

INDIAN TONIC - likely to be on plenty of lists. Won at Ascot and then finished second to Flashthecash at Cheltenham in April. Disappointed when beaten at Stratford (11-8 fav) off a mark of 109, but that should ensure he starts on a good handicap mark this season. Possibly unsuited by the track at Stratford, or maybe another ex-Irish import who needed more time to acclimatise. Jumps well, showed good form on soft and fast ground.

LIGHT VENEER - Had an excellent season as a novice without ever taking on the best horses until his final outing, when he was predictably outpaced over two and a half miles on fast ground. As a result he is likely to start the season on a fair handicap mark (117 at end of last season) and certainly has the scope to win off that mark. Suited by tough tracks - won at Exeter, Hexham and ran well at Towcester.

Both horses had already run and produced disappointing performances, which led to them being likely to start at a decent price. Light Veneer had finished fourth at Wincanton under top weight, but the downhill finish there was unlikely to suit him if my analysis was correct. Here he had bottom weight and had never been beaten over three miles or more by any horse who had to give him weight. The course was certain to suit him if I was right. Indian Tonic had run even worse when pulled up at Newton Abbot, but had weakened very quickly in the manner of a horse who had sustained an injury in running. Again he was likely to be better suited by this track if my analysis was correct.

I also felt that the likely favourites in this race all had weaknesses, which pointed to them being poor value. Flashthecash had fallen at Sandown six days earlier in a three-runner race and was badly weighted with my fancies on form from the spring. Washington Crossing had never raced over more than two and a half miles and Cheltenham provides a severe test of stamina. Native Pride came from a stable in excellent form, but hadn't raced since the previous January and lacked experience over fences.

On the day, Light Veneer was advertised at 12-1 and Indian Tonic at 16-1. With the doubt about the physical condition of Indian Tonic in view of his run at Newton Abbot, and the favourable stats for Light Veneer, he was my confident selection. As we will see later, I strongly favour the star horse in a small stable as the value bet.

On arrival at Cheltenham, I bet £3,600-300 with Tote Credit. After a check at the pre-parade ring, I went to Tatts and obtained one bet of £1,000-70 and two of £1,000-80 about Light Veneer, followed up with a £30 Reverse CSF in the course betting shop.

Indian Tonic led to the last, where Light Veneer took over and ran on up the hill to win by four lengths, with Indian Tonic holding second, five lengths clear of the remainder. Both were returned at an SP of 10-1. The CSF paid £87.15, and my total profit on the race came to just over £9,000.

My confidence remained intact despite the losing run, my capital allowed me to ride out the run and still have a 'proper' bet when the time was right; my calculation got me a better price than SP; and my cynicism enabled me to ignore the clarion calls of the experts for Flashthecash and Co.

Would that it were always so - but days like this can only be expected once or twice per year. To cap the story, a close friend was persuaded to include Light Veneer in his Jackpot and achieved a lifetime ambition and a return of £1900 for a £36 outlay.

Chapter Two

The right type - Flat

Given his success in recent years, it seems likely that most readers will have seen at least one of Linford Christie's 100 metre championship victories. All of these races have produced similar scenarios, with Christie storming through to overtake his rivals in the final third of the race, to win, usually going away at the finish. If you had to describe in a single word the quality that makes Christie successful, I suspect 'Power' would top the list of answers.

Used as a verb - as it frequently has been on these occasions by David Coleman - 'to power' is defined in my dictionary as 'to move in a powerful and vigorous manner'. That doesn't take us much further forward, but it does put it in a better context. Thus Coleman's exultant commentary cliche, 'Christie powers home', can be seen, adequately and accurately to describe the event.

If these 100 metre races were in fact horse races, it is much more likely that the cliche employed to describe Christie's performance, would be 'turn of foot'. This is the term regularly used to describe any race in which one horse puts distance between himself and his rivals in the closing stages.

It is a term which clearly suggests that the victory has been achieved as a result of acceleration, a sharp increase in speed which the horse's rivals have been unable to match. In this instance, in my view, the cliche neither adequately nor accurately describes the event.

Detailed analysis of Linford Christie's running has shown that his victories don't result from acceleration on his part, but from the fact that his ability and training allow him to maintain his top speed for longer than his rivals. When he appears to be 'powering home', he is simply maintaining a level speed whilst his rivals are slowing down.

Consideration of Christie's form at 200 metres gives credence to this view, since he is clearly unable to maintain his top speed for all of the extra distance and regularly fades in the last quarter of these races. Whilst he is a world class athlete at 100 metres, he isn't even certain of winning his national title at 200 metres.

Although it is easy to argue that a 100 metre foot race has no relevance when considering horse races over much longer distances, I feel the power Christie demonstrates is a prime quality to be sought for and recognised in identifying horses who can provide successful bets. It is the power to sustain increased speed that produces winners, rather than the more commonly identified ability to accelerate. Of course the two things together would guarantee success, but on the rare occasions this occurs (Shergar, Dancing Brave, Desert Orchid), then the world and his grandmother, and even the racing journalists, are able to spot the horse and any chance of value goes out of the window.

So, for me, it is this definable power that identifies the right type of horse - that is, the right type to produce future winners at decent prices. Defining 'power' is a good deal easier than putting into writing a clear picture of how I decide when watching a race that a horse has the quality for which I am looking.

To begin, let us consider Flat racing. The quality we are seeking will be demonstrated over the final two furlongs of a race, whatever the distance. It is in this part of most races that the average speed will increase and the horse with the power will be the one who sustains this increased speed over all, or at least most, of the quarter-mile. Our desired horse will gradually draw away from most of his rivals, as they slow down and he maintains his speed. Quite often two or three horses will draw away together and the weaker rivals will suddenly crack, ie. slow down; and as their jockeys sense defeat the gaps will grow quite suddenly. If two or three horses remain together through to the finish, then in all probability they are simply slowing down together, and others will close from behind. They may even be headed by a horse coming from behind.

Let us dispose here of two myths that litter the writing on horse racing in the press and in formbooks. Firstly, the horse who 'finishes fast', sometimes to win the race in the last strides, and sometimes to finish close up and apparently unlucky. Let us reverse the usual logic employed in this type of race and ask not why the horse was finishing fast, but why he got so far behind the leaders in the first place? In my view he got behind because he wasn't good enough to sustain the average speed being maintained by the leaders earlier in the race. He appears to finish fast, but, as we've established, it is much more likely that he is simply maintaining his speed (a speed insufficient for him to keep up) and that his rivals are slowing down dramatically in the final furlong. And the reason they are slowing down is that they are not good enough, or fit enough, to maintain the average speed they were able to attain at the two-furlong pole.

So myth number one is that horses who finish fast in the final furlong are horses to follow because they possess a turn of foot. Of course there will be occasions when this cliche is shown by future events to be correct. Indeed there are very rare horses who need to be ridden so that they only lead very near the finish, but note that these horses don't usually get left behind by the power horses two furlongs out, but follow them through, sustaining the same speed through the final two furlongs. But these horses rarely make good value bets as so much depends on their getting a clear run. It is much safer to assume that horses who finish fast are of limited interest, since they clearly couldn't attain the average speed of the other horses earlier in the race. And since fast finishers are given so much publicity, they invariably start at shorter odds than their form warrants.

The second myth is that horses who finish fast will automatically be suited by a longer trip in their future races. This theory seems attractive if we assume that the longer race will be run at a lower average speed, which will make it easier for the horse who got left behind at the pace of the shorter race. And as with other myths, there are enough cases where it proves to be true for it to maintain a hold over the press and the formbooks. In my view a horse who is unable to raise his speed in a one-mile race, will be just as likely to find the same problem at a mile and a quarter. To put it in the terms that this chapter addresses, he doesn't have the power, and the change of trip won't alter that basic fact. The likeliest exception here occurs in maiden races, where the opportunity to race over a longer trip may well produce the improvement the myth predicts, but once again the value is doubtful.

So the ideal pattern in a Flat race, to identify a horse with the power, is one who hits the front somewhere between the two-furlong mark and a point about 200 yards from the finish and then draws one or two lengths clear. It doesn't matter if other horses are closing in the final

100 yards - he has shown the power and they haven't. There may be more than one horse producing this pattern of performance in a race, although more than two should raise doubts about the quality of the race. Obviously they can't all win and those who are beaten after showing the power from two furlongs out, may well fade and be passed by our friends, the fast finishers. But remember they have duelled with the eventual winner and reached the limits of their ability - next time back them to beat the fast finishers.

In a small field our power horse may hit the front earlier, simply due to lack of competition, and a front runner who goes clear from a decent pace certainly fits the desired pattern. It is small fields and races with a slow pace that can cause problems in analysis, but any race in which more than half the field finish close up at the finish is suspect.

I should perhaps make it clear at this point that the overall class of a race is still the first consideration. If I identify a 'power' horse in a 0-80 handicap at Salisbury, I wouldn't back him to produce the same performance in a Group 3 race at Ascot. But I would certainly have him on my short list for a 0-90 handicap at the same venue.

To boil this theory down to a formula which can be applied using a standard formbook or trade paper, I basically prefer winners who lead more than a furlong from the finish, as well as horses who lead somewhere inside the final two furlongs but are headed before the finish, to horses who finish fast to snatch victory or who finish close up and in the frame. I expect horses who achieve this sort of performance in any race above 0-70 class to be able to win again in the same class and in most cases improve into higher class races.

To offer an example with which most readers will be familiar, consider the 1994 Derby and Oaks. The Derby winner, Erhaab, doesn't fit my power pattern, and in fact fits more closely into the fast-finisher mould. But the Oaks winner, Balanchine, clearly does fit the power pattern very well, having led over two out and fought off challengers before drawing away and holding off the fast finisher Wind In Her Hair.

The right type - National Hunt

The commentaries on jumping races are littered with comments about so and so losing half a length, or a length, with a slow jump. With only eight obstacles in a two-mile hurdle, and 12 in a two-mile chase, this would suggest certain limits on the amount of ground which could be gained or lost at the jumps.

And yet, when Desert Orchid ran in the Sagaro Stakes over two miles on the Flat at Ascot, he finished tailed off, beaten too far for the form book to offer an accurate assessment of the distance. Since the first two home in that race (Ascot Gold Cup winners Longboat and Gildoran) understandably never ran over hurdles, it can't be dogmatically stated that Desert Orchid would have beaten them in a two-mile hurdle, but I think we can all guess who would have started favourite.

We can, however, draw a comparison with the fifth finisher in that Sagaro Stakes, Asir, who went on to win the Sun Alliance Novices Hurdle almost a year later. His Timeform NH rating of 159, based on that win, was the same as the rating given to Desert Orchid for the hurdle season prior to his run on the Flat. So, in the view of Timeform, they were of equal merit over hurdles, but clearly Asir was much the better on the Flat.

The reason is that quick and accurate jumping makes a far greater difference than the 'gained a length' type of comment would suggest. Watching a jump race on television, or from the nether reaches of the Members Stand, it is impossible to get an accurate picture of the effect jumping has on the outcome of a race. With good binoculars at certain tracks where the fences are at right angles to the watcher (Kempton and Warwick are the two best examples in the south), it is easier to see how much ground can be gained or lost. But for real understanding, you have to get close to the action, out on the course, preferably two or three fences from the finish.

Only then will you see how some horses slow down to adjust their stride pattern, how some accelerate and attack the fence with gusto, and how others simply take off and hope for the best. You will also see how some horses quickly regain their natural stride pattern, whilst others take several strides to recover their balance and momentum.

Half a dozen trips into the country and you shouldn't need convincing about the rest of this piece - good jumpers win most jump races.

The right type in a NH race jumps cleanly and quickly in the early and middle stages of a race, and will often be seen to be gaining ground at the obstacles before being reined back by his rider. In the closing stages he will continue to jump tidily, even if tired, and if asked by his rider will respond with a big jump at the final fence or hurdle. Because he has not used up his energy by constantly having to re-accelerate to cruising speed after slowing at the obstacles, he will have resources left for the finish to enable him to gallop all the way to the line. In other words he will show the same sort of power that I favour in a Flat race.

If you see one of these paragons in a novice event, you have a potential goldmine. If you see one in a low-grade or novice handicap, better still, as the right type of jumper can overcome almost any weight rise the handicapper can throw at him (e.g. Kings Fountain, Tipping Tim, Gambling Royal, Docklands Express, Floyd).

In its novice days this type of horse can still be a faller, but it will usually be as a result of over-jumping, or over-exuberance, rather than the type of clumsy, or tired fall that is associated with the wrong type. As they gain experience they are much less likely to fall, and will rarely make any serious mistakes.

Two things to remember: a skilled jumper of hurdles will not automatically be as good over fences, as the required technique is very different; and secondly, always be wary after a horse has had a lay-off through injury. Bad legs or a bad back may prevent a natural jumper from reproducing his previous form, so wait until you've seen the evidence.

Chapter Three

Information

The greatest change in racing in the 30 years of my involvement is in the volume and detail of the information available to the serious punter. The biggest transformation has come about with the advent of the domestic video recorder and the subsequent introduction of SIS providing TV pictures of the majority of racing staged in this country. Whereas 15 years ago mainstream television provided the only pictures of racing, and home recording was impossible for the man in the street, I am now able to watch, record and re-watch around 90 per cent of the races run each year.

The written information has also gained in detail, with press and form organisations able to take advantage of race pictures to provide more detailed reports than were ever possible when everything had to be absorbed from a single live viewing. The detail provided in the racing trade press for each meeting would also amaze a reader transported forward from 20 years ago, thanks to the gains from computerised printing and the ability to hold form on a computer database.

The challenge for the professional punter is to sift all this information and to place his own interpretation on it, in order to maintain an edge over his source of income. I personally use the following sources, but make no recommendation as to their advantage or otherwise over alternative services:

Sporting Life delivered daily

Sporting Life Weekender delivered weekly

Timeform Perspective delivered twice weekly

SIS Daily Racing Review - a nightly transmission of all races shown that day in the betting shops, lasting up to 90 minutes.

The total annual cost approaches £2,000!

I record the SIS programmes and keep a library covering the racing for the current season, either NH or Flat. These tapes allow me to review races when I'm preparing for a meeting, and I also use them on a Sunday to review the events of the past week. Since so many organisations now watch these films, it is unlikely that I'll spot anything they have missed, but it does allow me to put a value on the merit of a particular performance. There is no doubt that seeing a race, even with the drawbacks of TV coverage, is more informative than anything you can read about it.

Another valuable source of information, and one that should come as no surprise to any serious punter, is my own record of my bets. Apart from the maintenance of accounts, these provide a vital historical record which can be analysed to discover strengths and weaknesses in my betting patterns.

For example, my records, which stretch back 11 years in their current format, tell me I'm very profitable in long distance handicaps - the Ascot Stakes over two and a half miles is my favourite Flat race - but that if the Premier League were a sprint handicap, I'd probably have had a maximum bet on Ipswich!

Since in my previous life I spent 25 years working in and around computer operations, it may come as a surprise to discover that I don't use a PC to keep records or to analyse races or form. What those 25 years taught me, if nothing else, was the truth of a standard computer adage - GIGO: garbage in, garbage out. They also taught me that getting accurate data into a computer was a slow and mind-numbingly boring process. Personally I prefer the computer nature provided me with - the one that understands instinct, hunch, feel and plain old-fashioned luck.

If I may digress for a computer story - I did once write a computer program based on race times as a test program in my early days at IBM in the mid-sixties. To keep the keypunching of data to a manageable level, I dealt only with two-year-old races over five and six furlongs. For each horse, I stored data on the last three runs when finishing in the first six. To analyse a race I entered the name of each runner via a typewriter console, and the program basically did a Timeform, and then printed a predicted result, a process that took around fifteen minutes for a ten-runner race!

The program produced a famous success when it predicted that Mountain Call would win a race at Ascot, on a day in September when a party from the office was going racing. The printout gave the horse a ten-length advantage. It won easily at 11-2 (I think) and the party returned to London much the worse for wear. I never did tell the others that the prediction owed much to the fact that my database contained no records for the Vincent O'Brien-trained odds-on favourite - ignorance is sometimes bliss, even for a computer program!

I'm sure that many readers, seeing the title of this chapter, anticipated a treatise on the necessity of maintaining a string of stable contacts to provide so-called inside information. I'm well aware that many serious punters regard this sort of information as essential, and indeed use it as the mainspring of their betting operation.

Having read my comments earlier on the limited value of the views of trainers and jockeys, it should come as no surprise that I personally hold information from stable staff and gallop watchers in even lower esteem. From my own personal involvement as an owner, I'm well aware that the views of stable staff on the horses in their care are likely to be as subjective as those of a mother commenting on her children.

It is also true that my preferred area of operations is one in which such inside information is of little use, since I almost never bet in two-year-old maiden races, or on unraced maidens at three-years old. I prefer to stick to betting on what I have seen for myself, rather than betting on what someone else tells me they have seen.

30 . Against The Crowd

Chapter Four

Form and race analysis

The average punter confronted with a ten-runner race will settle down with whatever form guide he uses, and start looking for the winner. I used the same method for many years, and like everyone else I found my share of winners. As a method it suffers from two main failings:

The selections are likely to be exactly the same as those made by most punters, and by newspaper tipsters.

If the second horse in the list looks like a winner, the analysis of the remaining runners is inevitably coloured.

My own method nowadays reverses the standard logic and concentrates on the fact that every ten-runner race must include nine losers. As I analyse the form of each runner, I concentrate on looking for reasons why they won't win, rather than reasons why they will. Not surprisingly, these reasons are much easier to find!

As I work through a race, I write brief notes, with comments on the negatives for those who are likely to lose. These will cover such things as incorrect trip, unsuitable going, stable out of form, unsuited by track, too high in handicap, outclassed, out of form, poor jumper, etc, etc. As anyone who has listened to a jockey and trainer after a race will know, the list of reasons for not winning is endless.

Those who cannot be eliminated are placed on a short list for further consideration. For horses on this short list, I'm likely to view films of their recent races as well as re-reading the form book. I also make an assessment of the sort of price I'd expect to see offered about each of these short-listed runners.

If the short list consists of one horse, then either I've got the analysis wrong, or I've simply identified an odds-on favourite. If, however, the one horse is a value price (more on this thorny topic later), then a probable bet has been identified.

If the short list contains more than four names, then it is probable that the race is simply too competitive to be considered as a betting event.

At this stage (usually the day before the race), I don't try to reduce a short list of two, three or four down to a specific selection. The information available in the immediate pre-race process of the parade and the canter to post, as well as the offered prices in the ring, could produce a decision as to which offers the best bet. The key statement is 'offers the best bet', which is not the same as saying 'offers the best chance of winning'.

To demonstrate the process, let's look at the two-mile, one-furlong handicap staged at Bath on Saturday, 11 June 1994. The notes below are those I wrote when studying this race on the previous afternoon. The first figure given for each horse is the handicap mark for this race.

75 **RUNAWAY PETE** - *seasonal debut. Stable in form. Untried beyond 1³/₄m. Poor form last 2 starts last yr, including wl btn in a claimer. Was getting 7lb from Hill of Dreams when 4th to him over 13f here last summer, so now 13lb worse off. Small sort with little scope for improvement at 4-y-o.*

70 **HAITHAM** - *4-11 15f hcp Warwick good-soft off 70, btn 5l. Off course a long time prior to that run. Stays trip OK and has won at 2¹/₂m. Fast ground unlikely to suit after injury and looks too high in hcp.*

69 **HILL OF DREAMS** - *won muddling 14f hcp Haydock good off 64 - most of other runners got in each other's way as he went clear. Prev 2-16 1¹/₂m Pontefract off 63. Untried beyond 14f. Generally modest form last yr, but often in better class than this - more consistent this yr. Short list.*

68 **HARLESTONE BROOK** - *2-7 2m hcp Ripon good-soft off 66, btn 6l by Ritto, with Taroudant 8l bhd in 3rd. Just bhd Hill of Dreams on seasonal debut over 14f, at level weights. Also ran bhd that horse here last summer over 13f, btn ¹/₂l when getting 7lb. Off course since mid April. From a strong staying family. Goes OK on fast ground. Short list.*

51 **HORIZON** - *moderate front runner. Been running on AW tracks, where he was rated 78 at start of yr. Wl btn on turf last season, last time 9-12 in a hcp off 55. Looks easy to bt away from the sand and stable in no sort of form.*

*46 **HOT OFF THE PRESS** - 6-10 2m hcp Ripon good off 45, having prev won a 2m seller at Catterick! Outclassed and too high in hcp.*

*44 **SARAZAR** - 5-16 in dire 2m hcp Folkestone off 45. Long lay-off prior to that. Obv difficult to train and still a maiden.*

Remaining 3 runners are well out of the handicap and are completely outclassed.

Short List

Hill Of Dreams - in form, fit, stable going well, stamina doubt as a son of very fast 1m winner Forest Flower.

Harlestone Brook - almost certain to stay, and prev form puts him close to H O D at shorter trips. Lay-off since April suggests a problem.

Having written these notes, I didn't expect to have a bet on this race, as I estimated that these two would start at around 6-4 and 2-1 respectively.

On the day, paddock inspection showed Hill Of Dreams looking well, but Harlestone Brook was sweating slightly and didn't look 100 per cent right in his coat. However, on the way to post Hill Of Dreams seemed ill at ease on the fast ground (though Timeform had noted him as a poor mover when he had run well), but Harlestone Brook went down extremely well, showing a long, flowing stride.

In the market, Hill Of Dreams had shortened from 6-4 to 11-10 and Harlestone Brook had drifted from 7-2 to 5-1. Given all the evidence, instinct (hard to define, but all important) pointed to a bet on Harlestone Brook as the value in an apparent two-horse race. A bet of £1,500-300 was obtained and Harlestone Brook was returned 9-2.

The result - well it doesn't really matter, since the purpose of the example is to demonstrate the method. But in this case virtue earned its reward, with Harlestone Brook winning from Runaway Pete, with Hill Of Dreams well beaten and reported as a non-stayer by connections at the subsequent enquiry.

Twenty years ago I would almost certainly have marked Hill Of Dreams as a 'cert' and backed him regardless of price. After the race I would have blamed the jockey, the horse, the going - almost anything except myself for a wrong decision.

Ten years ago I would still have seen Hill Of Dreams as a cert, but I would have been able to resist a bet at such a short price. After the race I would have experienced a glow of pleasure at avoiding a loser, but would still have been able to offer reasons why nobody in his right mind could have backed the winner - off course for two months, drifted in the betting, etc.

Who knows where another ten years' experience might lead!

I carry out this process of form study and note-taking for most races at the meetings I plan to attend, usually excluding only those races which are outside my current betting rules. It is important to realise, however, that doing the work on a race doesn't necessarily mean I will make a bet, or that I will know on the morning of the race exactly what bets I'll place that afternoon. The form study provides an essential background against which later information can be measured before deciding on a bet.

As in the example above, I didn't plan a bet on Harlestone Brook, but when I saw the horses going to post and the state of the betting market, I knew enough to be confident that 5-1 was a value price. Without the advance form study, the later information wouldn't be sufficient to compel a bet.

For races in which I don't bet, the form study allows me to put the actual result into perspective i.e. was it what I had expected or was it a surprise? If it was an unexpected result, I'll go back to the formbook that evening to see if I can find what I missed first time around.

In other words, reading form provides the essential background information, the framework on which all my betting is based. To coin a topical parallel, to the average TV viewer, the news and pictures from the civil wars in Yugoslavia are inexplicable in modern day Europe. But to anyone who has read and studied the history of the region (i.e. read the Balkan formbook), the current fighting is both predictable and understandable.

Chapter Five

Strategy

The Kitchi Koo principle

On 9 January 1993, whilst most punters and racing followers were concentrating on the Mildmay Chase at Sandown, where Rushing Wild established himself as a Gold Cup contender, I was racing at Warwick. I travelled in company with a close friend and fellow punter, and over the journey we discussed the races.

We had both identified the two-mile, four furlong Whitlenge Handicap Hurdle as a likely betting race, with a dodgy favourite and a couple of other runners likely to be supported who we felt could be ignored. Independently, we had identified Kitchi Koo as a possible value outsider. Trained by Jim Wilson, the mare had won a similar race on heavy ground two seasons ago and had been lightly raced since. In two runs this season she had shown some promise when a staying-on fourth over course and distance, and we were prepared to forgive her a modest performance since at Chepstow, a course whose undulations don't suit all horses.

Although she was out of the handicap, she was on much the same mark as her earlier Warwick run, and was ridden by the same 7lb claimer - neither of us had ever heard of him. We agreed that in a weak race she could be worth a bet at around 16-1. I offered up Jailbreaker as the likeliest winner from amongst the main contenders, though admitting to an inevitable bias having had a substantial win when the same horse won a juvenile handicap at Newbury at 14-1 two years earlier.

In the race, Kitchi Koo got up close home to beat Jailbreaker, with the favourite seven lengths back in third. The starting price of the winner was 25-1. Neither of us had placed a bet on the race.

Now I'm aware that most punters can describe a similar experience, and you can choose to believe this one or not - the only person who matters in this story knows it is true. The difference is that I've taken the example to heart and it is now enshrined into my overall betting strategy, and is known as the Kitchi Koo Principle.

And the principle is that if as a result of your form analysis, you can make a good argument for supporting a long shot, then you must make a bet. The key factor is that no bet on such a horse can be expected to fulfil the same exacting criteria that you would apply to a 4-1 shot. There are bound to be ifs and buts about such a selection, otherwise it wouldn't be 25-1 (or 12-1 either).

Often these ifs and buts will include an unknown claiming rider, a small or apparently out-of-form stable, a horse running from out of the handicap, a poor run in its latest race, etc. But in races with poor favourites, and other runners who are out of form or too high in the handicap, or running over the wrong trip, or on the wrong ground, these are the bets that separate the plodder from the truly successful punter.

It is these bets that most clearly mark out the punter who is betting 'Against The Crowd'.

Of course you cannot hope to make these sort of bets pay if you back horses simply because they are outsiders. The vast majority of horses offered at 20-1 or more by bookmakers have absolutely no chance of winning, and should realistically be priced at 100-1 or better. Finding the value bets from amongst the tens of thousands of outsiders who run every year requires constant study of the form book, and inexhaustible patience to wait for the right opportunity.

They also emphasise two of the 'Four Cs' described earlier. It is inevitable that a high percentage of bets on such horses will be losers, and the losing runs can be long. Confidence and Capital are the requirements to survive the losing runs.

My personal strategy mixes these long-shot bets in with my more orthodox day-to-day bets at shorter prices. These provide the regular action and profits to sustain the operation. Over a sufficient period of time (two to three years), I expect the short-price bets to produce sufficient profits to at least cover all the stakes lost on long-shot bets, leaving the successful long-shot bets to provide pure profit.

To demonstrate how this works in principle, let's look at my betting record for 1993. During this calendar year I had 48 bets in which the price I obtained was 10-1 or better and I categorise these as the long-shot bets. The potential return on these bets varied from £2,000 up to £9,000, dependent on price and my degree of confidence in the selection, and in one or two cases how much I could get on before the value disappeared. Backing a 14-1 shot to win £4,000 at Ludlow on the Monday before Christmas requires a degree of subtlety!

These 48 bets produced only five winners, the first of which came on June 15, after a run of 28 losers. However, by the end of the year, these bets showed a profit of £8,620 on a turnover of £14,480. A full list of the long-shot bets and their results is included as Appendix 1.

After 28 losing bets I had lost stakes to the total of £7,900 on long shots but, as planned within the strategy, my profits on shorter-price bets had kept my overall deficit at that point to £1,900 for the calendar year.

Apart from their desirable effect on profits, nothing can beat the feeling of pulling off a big win on an outsider. The glow that ensues will last for days, even weeks, and produce a feeling of confidence that can have a beneficial impact on your betting.

Specialisation

There are now over 7,000 horse races run each year in this country. Nobody, even with the help of computers, can hope to keep track of so many races, so many horses, or so much form. To have any chance of profitable betting, you must concentrate your efforts onto a smaller number of horses and fewer races.

Your personal choice of specialisation is almost irrelevant - doubtless there are punters for whom selling handicap hurdles are amongst life's greatest pleasures, just as there are those who swear by the much discussed and much analysed Group 1 races on the Flat. To me the first of these is simply unfathomable, and the second rarely offers any edge to the professional.

My own specialisation operates in two ways. Firstly, I bet only on course at the 150-160 meetings I attend each year. This instantly reduces my range to around 1,000 races, and eliminates those horses who operate solely in the north of England and across the border. Secondly, I mostly limit my betting at those meetings to the longer races, i.e. those at seven furlongs or longer on the Flat, and those at two and a half miles or longer over the jumps.

The reasons for my choices are simple - my betting records show quite clearly that I'm hopeless at assessing form and value in shorter races. And they also show that in the long term I cannot hope to profit from off-course betting, so long as betting tax remains at ten per cent.

By betting only on course I benefit from my experience at viewing horses in the paddock, and watching them move to post. It would require a separate book, or better still a video, to describe what can be learned from these parts of the pre-race process, and I can offer no encouragement to the novice punter when I say that it will take many years' practice before you can hope to spot what the experienced observer will see instinctively. I can only say that the effort will be worthwhile - I now find more poor favourites in the ten minutes before the off than I do in the hours spent with the form book and the video.

However, I have been saved the task of writing such a book because *The Winning Look* by Nick Mordin covers the subject of paddock watching far better than anything I could hope to produce (see Appendix 4 for details).

Rules

It is now my practice at the start of each new season (Flat and NH), to write down the rules for my betting strategy, to carry them with me, and to re-read them regularly to remind me of the object of the exercise. From personal experience I know how easy it is to become bored or distracted and to start looking for bets simply to provide some action. The written rules are simply an attempt at re-imposing discipline whenever that temptation arises.

For the 1994 Flat season the rules read as follows - I've included a brief explanation where necessary:

1 Stick to single win bets.

2 Maintain a 2-1 minimum price limit.

3 Think twice at under 4-1.

4 Concentrate on races at a mile plus.

5 Ignore all 2-y-o races except at the Festivals - in other words limit 2-y-o bets to the group races where I've had some success in past seasons.

6   Let the first race go by - this allows a chance to observe the going and any effect of the draw, especially where the weather has recently changed.

7   No bets is no problem.

8   Concentrate always on the Festivals.

9   Be prepared to travel to back one horse - it's cheaper to drive to Goodwood, for example, than to pay tax on a £300 bet.

10 Remember to check the Tote win pool on the big days.

11 Keep it simple before Royal Ascot.

12 Stick to your guns.

13 Consider a bet in all the Big 30 handicaps.

14 Stop after Ascot Festival day - end of September.

Nothing very original or revolutionary in that lot, but as most punters will know only too well, it's easy to lose your way and start making bets you will regret as soon as you get home and carry out your record keeping. And it's equally easy, and just as annoying, to miss a bet for reasons which will look illogical in the cold light of 20/20 hindsight.

The Big 30

This is referred to above in rule 13 for the Flat. It is simply a list of 30 major handicaps, run at one mile or longer, ranging through the season from the Newbury Spring Cup to the November Handicap. These are races that I either avoided as being too difficult to bother with, or in which I backed a rank outsider in a futile search for value. A recent rethink has marked these races as good betting opportunities, and they form a worthwhile part of my strategy.

All of these races (they are listed in full in Appendix 2) attract competitive fields of good horses. Studying these races will always prove worthwhile, even if no bet results from the analysis, simply because these races are the most competitive, and therefore tend to produce winners elsewhere. And despite the big fields, they frequently produce results which can be analysed correctly, and winners that offer good value bets in the 5-1 to 12-1 range.

There are also patterns within these races, whereby horses will appear in more than one of the races, and form will hold good from one contest to the next. I think there are two factors at work here:

The bigger fields produce more crowding.

The races are run at a true pace throughout.

These factors count against the impressive winner in a smaller field, who can't hold his position so easily and can't produce the same finishing power off a stronger pace.

The horse who first opened my eyes to these factors, and the value of betting in these races, was Sky Cloud, who followed a win in the seven-furlong Victoria Cup with success in the Golden Mile at Goodwood (20-1), and later in the major mile-handicap on St Leger day at 10-1. The bigger the field, and the more competitive the race, the better he seemed to run.

One final pointer in favour of betting on these races is that many of them can be simplified by taking the effect of the draw into the calculations - once again the big fields emphasise the advantage gained from a favourable draw.

Chapter Six

The market

One of the commonest sights in the betting ring at any racecourse is the punter who is rushing around, pushing and shoving anyone who stands in his way, trying to obtain 11-10 for his money, when the general offer about the favourite is Evens. If he manages this feat, he is convinced he has obtained value, regardless of whether his selection wins or loses. In fact if his selection wins, his gain is equal to one-tenth of his unit stake.

My strategy of seeking longer-price winners means that the average starting price of my selections is around 6-1. But the key to making a profit on these selections lies in obtaining a better price than that in the ring. If the horse is offered at 7-1 at some point in the betting, then by taking that price, a winning selection will mean that my gain is equal to a whole unit stake. Using my average £300 stake, my bet gains me £300 profit greater than the SP, whereas my theoretical favourite backer only gains £30. To make up the difference, his strike-rate would have to be ten times better than mine.

Of course there will be occasions when he will be able to obtain 6-5, 5-4 or perhaps even more about his Evens winner, but equally there will be times when I can get 8-1. In addition, I have a further edge, since I can make use of the course bookmakers' willingness to 'lay the fractions' to backers employing large stakes. Even if my 6-1 winner is never offered at a longer price, I can place bets of £1,000-160 on course, which equates to a real price of 6.25-1. These fractions are available at all prices above 5-1 and should always be requested by on-course backers. If the bookmaker declines, then withhold your bet and try elsewhere. (For table of fractions see overleaf.)

As you can see, the benefit of taking these fractions varies, but at 6-1, 8-1, 12-1 and 16-1, the additional profit is well worthwhile, and considerably greater than the margin obtained by our favourite backer.

Returning to my 6-1 shot on offer at 7-1. How can I tell that the 7-1 will disappear and that 6-1 will be the returned price for SP backers?

Table of Fractions

11-2	1,000-180	or	500-90	
6-1	1,000-160	or	500-80	6.25-1
13-2	1,000-150	or	500-75	
7-1	1,000-140	or	500-70	
8-1	1,000-120	or	500-60	8.33-1
9-1	1,000-110	or	500-55	
11-1	1,000-90	or	500-45	
12-1	1,000-80	or	500-40	12.50-1
114-1	1,000-70	or	500-35	
16-1	1,000-60	or	500-30	16.66-1

How can I be sure that the price won't extend to 15-2 or even 8-1 if I wait a little longer? Well, the answer is that I can't be sure, but that experience and the use of some quick mental arithmetic will improve my chances of making the right decision. This is where the calculation part of the four C's comes into play.

Let's assume this mythical 6-1 winner is in a six-runner race. When I first go into the ring, I check the theoretical profit margin for the bookies, based on the best prices currently showing. For example:

Good Thing	Evens	50%
Hopeful	11-4	27%
Possible	9-2	18%
My Fancy	6-1	14%
No Real Chance	14-1	7%
Rank Outsider	33-1	3%
Total		**119%**

So the current margin is 19 per cent, but I know that the SP is likely to represent something closer to ten to 14 per cent. Thus there is the potential for a five to nine per cent improvement in the prices offered. For My Fancy to move from 6-1 to 7-1 represents a significant difference for me as a backer in terms of my likely profit, but in terms of the bookmaker margin it is a change of less than two per cent. If the five to nine per cent easing of the prices is evenly spread across the six runners, it is very likely that at least some of the course bookmakers will offer 7-1. With an even spread the revised prices would be:

Good Thing	11-10	48%
Hopeful	3-1	25%
Possible	5-1	16%
My Fancy	7-1	12%
No Real Chance	20-1	5%
Rank Outsider	33-1	3%
Total		**109%**

This gives the bookies a final margin of nine per cent, which is a little low, but certainly possible. In practice it is much more likely that the mass of mug punters will decide that either Good Thing or Hopeful is the business, resulting in either an odds-on favourite, or a 9-4 second favourite. For my purposes it doesn't really matter what happens to the other prices, except that I'm waiting for the moment when the margin has been stretched as low as possible, as that is the moment to step in and place my bet. In other words if the prices listed above are offered, then the margin has dropped to nine per cent and a further easing of prices is unlikely. At this point, even if backers like me make no move, it is likely that the agents of the betting shop chains will step in and attempt to adjust the market in their favour. Personally I have no objection to this practice, which seems to me to be an entirely logical way to run their businesses, and since their efforts are mainly confined to the favourites they don't affect my work at all.

Obviously this sort of calculation is much harder to do when you are confronted by a 16-runner handicap, but I find that you can still obtain the necessary feel for the state of the market by concentrating your maths on those horses priced at 10-1 or lower, which will inevitably attract the bulk of the business.

One final point to note here is that the sort of margins discussed above are unlikely to arise at a lesser track on a busy day - such as a Bank Holiday or a summer Saturday. The course bookmakers will treat these days as their 'make money' days, and prices will be restricted accordingly. No blame can be attached to the layers, since the mugs will still swarm all around them fighting to get their money on, almost regardless of the lack of value on offer. I generally stay at home on Bank Holidays!

So the first key to making a profit in the market is to try always to take the best price offered. The importance of this can be seen from my analysis of my own racecourse bets in 1993, which produced a profit of £15,200. The same bets placed at SP would have produced a profit of £8,200, and if placed off course with tax paid on, a loss of £3,000. Beating the market means the difference between a fair living and a struggle, and the expense of going racing is easily justified.

You will be aware that I've made no mention of using bookmakers' early prices as a means of obtaining the best odds. I have occasionally used these for off-course bets, but only where I am entirely certain in my own mind that by doing so I will substantially beat the price I can get on course, with the difference being sufficient to cover the off-course tax. The question of the ability to get on also arises - my own experience is that it is easiest to do so on major races or at the major Festivals and I very rarely use early prices elsewhere.

We hear much from John McCririck on C4 about his beloved 'steamers', especially when they happen to oblige, but a more reasoned analysis of early price races will show that the winners are just as often available at an equal or longer price on course than was offered in the betting shop at 10.00 a.m.

On the subject of 'getting on', I'm aware that most 'professionals' offer details of closed credit accounts as a badge of their success. I cannot join their ranks, having avoided the problem of the closed account by the simple device of never opening one with any of the big three. I do have an account with Tote Credit, which I use for bets at away courses, and for taking an early price on course, and I've had several big wins without any problems.

Value in the Market

In recent seasons I have slowly increased the odds below which I will not bet, from a position of never betting odds-on, to my current rule of never betting below 2-1. With increasing experience I'm likely to push this barrier higher in future.

Apart from the fact that it is very difficult to make decent profits on short-priced horses, I feel that the backer of such animals is up against the sheer unpredictability of horses, often described in the phrase 'horses aren't machines'. Even if the punter has successfully analysed a race and identified the likeliest winner, taking into account all the factors known to him (e.g. form, ground, distance, draw, trainer, jockey, etc.), he can still be beaten by those things which can go wrong, but which he cannot foresee. Consider the following list of excuses for beaten horses:

- *went lame*
- *burst a blood vessel*
- *swallowed his tongue*
- *spread a plate*
- *filly in season*
- *got the 'virus'*

None of these can be predicted prior to a race, but all can happen just as easily to an odds-on favourite as to a 33-1 outsider - and the above list is by no means complete, since it doesn't include accidents in running, such as slow starts and interference. Personally, I estimate that around one-quarter of the 50,000+ runners each season are thus affected during a race - the percentage is probably higher over the jumps and lower in Flat races. If we put this into betting terms, then it is only 1-3 that your selection will complete a race in a condition that enables it to give of its best.

I've taken this argument one stage further, taking the view that a single win bet can really be seen as a win double. The first leg of the double is that your selection is correct, and the second leg is that the horse completes the race fit and well. Thus if the total return on your bet is Evens, the prices for the double are 1-3 'fit and well' and 1-2 'correct selection'. In other words, to break even with bets at Even money, your rate of correct selection has to be two out of three.

I'm sure most readers will question whether as many as 25 per cent are really affected by outside influences, but I'm equally sure they will agree that some sort of percentage figure for this factor should be taken into account. If you've never backed a short-priced horse who ran unaccountably badly, and appeared to return to form in later races, then you should be writing a book revealing your secret!

Whatever percentage you set, there is a bias that has to be overcome and which can be reflected in the 'win double' formula. The purpose of this piece is to point out that if you back longer-priced runners, then the second leg of the double assumes less importance as the price of your selections rises. For example, if the total return is 10-1, then the prices for the double are 1-3 'fit and well' and approximately 7-1 'correct selection'. To me, finding 10-1 winners at a rate of one in eight sounds much easier than finding Even-money winners at a rate of two in three. My preference for betting at longer prices is based on this theory, and on the success I've had in practice.

I've analysed my records for the four years 1990 - 1993 and listed all the single win bets where the price obtained fell in the range 9-1 to 11-1, with an average close to 10-1. In total there were 110 bets, which produced 17 winners. On a turnover of £30,000, the net profit was £24,450, which equates to better than 80 per cent. To produce the same percentage level of profit from 110 bets at Even-money, using level stakes, would require the backer to find 99 winners!

If is also much easier to find prices offered which provide a real edge over the market amongst the longer-priced horses. I can regularly obtain 10-1 in the ring about a horse which will be returned 8-1, and which will never be shown higher than 8-1 in a betting shop, because the 10-1 appears only on one or two boards and is taken before the price can be spotted and transmitted. For the level-stake punter, obtaining 10-1 about a general 8-1 shot has exactly the same effect on profits as obtaining 4-1 about a 2-1 shot. But whereas the former can be achieved about most 8-1 winners, the latter might happen once or twice a year.

As a final plus for the longer-priced selection, it is easier to get on. Most course bookmakers are happy to lay longer-priced horses to help balance their books, in which most money goes on to the first and second favourites. More often than not, I am paid out with a smile, since the races on which I win are also the ones on which they win.

Let me end this chapter by entering a plea on behalf of that much maligned group - Britain's racecourse bookmakers. I've been betting in Tattersalls for 30 years and I can truthfully say that in all that time I have never been treated with anything other than total honesty. The number of disputes I've had can be counted on one finger, and that was resolved amicably without recourse to officialdom. Whenever I've had problems with the handling of my financial affairs, they have always been with banks, building societies, insurance companies and the like - never with a racecourse bookmaker.

If you wish to be a serious on-course punter, treat the bookmakers with respect and you will be served in the same coin.

48 . Against The Crowd

Chapter Seven

Value

Since the publication of the best-selling book *Value Betting*, the concept of value in betting has been at the forefront of much of the writing and discussion on horse racing. Indeed, even the more conservative television pundits have recognised the trend - sadly their usage on air reveals only too clearly that, for most of them, 'value in betting' is still as mysterious an idea as 'truth in politics'.

To dismiss two of their more common statements, let's be clear that value cannot automatically be associated with any horse starting at a longer price than the favourite. And neither is there any such thing, in my view anyway, as a good value each-way bet. This second phrase seems to be used about almost any horse at 10-1 or more who moves into camera shot. Thus the speaker avoids uttering the probable truth that anyone who has backed the beast in question needs an immediate frontal lobotomy.

Returning to the more solid ground of the real world, I'm sure no serious punter would argue with the simple definition that value is in the eye of the beholder. What seems a value bet to me will look like an appalling waste of money to another punter - to coin a cliche, 'it's the difference of opinion that makes racing'.

In other words there is no such thing as A value bet, there is only MY value bet and YOUR value bet, because the recognition of value is a matter of personal opinion. MY value bet is achieved whenever I obtain a price which represents odds greater than my estimate of a horse's chance of winning a race. MY arrogance persuades me that this circumstance arises every time I have a bet - it is essential to my professional standing and morale that I believe it to be so. Inevitably, the benefit of hindsight will frequently show me to be wrong, usually within minutes! The only true measure of my ability to assess value comes at the end of each season when I close my accounts.

Leaving theory aside, how do I actually go about the search for value? There are three key ways, each discussed below.

Reducing the margin

Information supplied with the results printed in the trade press nowadays includes the SP percentage for each race - i.e. the bookmakers' theoretical profit margin on the race. The figure will vary from around 105 per cent in small fields, up to 160 per cent or even more in big fields. If the figure for any race dropped to 100 per cent this would mean (theoretically) a return of all stakes to backers of the winner with no profit or loss for the bookmaker.

My first method of value-seeking involves the search for races where I can reduce the margin to a figure significantly below 100 per cent, thereby tipping the market in my favour as a backer. The most common way of achieving this end is to discover bad favourites, either via form book study, or via racecourse inspection in the parade or the canter to post.

If I can eliminate a 6-4 favourite as having no realistic chance of winning, then a 110 per cent market changes to a 70 per cent market. At this point any bet I make on the race is a value bet, regardless of the price obtained, since the price would be much shorter if the 6-4 favourite were a non-runner.

Of course, if I can dismiss a 6-4 favourite so lightly, you might think that most other punters would be able to achieve the same thing, but the fact is that races like this arise every day. If a horse is forecast at 6-4 in the papers, it will quite likely start 6-4, even if it is sweating in the parade ring and then goes to post like a giraffe with corns, because betting shop punters know nothing of these events and the Big Three will move the market to reflect what happens in their shops.

And, just as often, horses go off as short-priced favourites despite potential problems that will convince some backers that no price would persuade them to support such an animal. If you doubt this, remember the Cheltenham Gold Cup for which Carvill's Hill started an Even-money favourite. Most of the serious punters of my acquaintance were convinced that this horse had little or no chance of putting in a clear round at Cheltenham, and that the race offered a great value opportunity, since eliminating the favourite reduced the margin to around 60 per cent.

At a much lower level the principle can be demonstrated quite clearly by considering the two-and-a-half-mile novice chase at

Worcester on 7 May 1994. The 5-4 favourite in this race was Unholy Alliance, trained by the in-form Kim Bailey, and the long odds-on winner of his last two races. How could anyone make a case to oppose such a horse? Well, those professionals who had seen his third-last race at Stratford had watched him throw away victory by stopping on the run-in and allowing the beaten Hillwalk to re-pass him close home. His two subsequent wins had been achieved unchallenged against weak opposition. Here he faced Castle Diamond, also a multiple winner during the current season and a horse who showed his taste for a battle when winning by a short head at Warwick under today's rider, Richard Dunwoody. Castle Diamond touched 5-1 before closing in to 7-2 at the off, whereas Unholy Alliance never exceeded 11-8 in the ring. Only three other runners started at less than 20-1. Which one would you want to be on - which one is value?

Well, after this race, the mugs were queueing up for their next pint of lager and questioning Norman Williamson's parentage, whilst the professionals went to collect. Of course it won't always work that way, but then again at 5-1 it doesn't have to! The fact is that bad favourites can be found every day that racing takes place.

Reducing the field

This method depends on using purely mechanical means to reduce the number of horses to be considered when analysing the form for a race. By far the commonest method I use is to eliminate half or more of the runners by using the draw, before I even start work with the formbook. There are plenty of races where this method can be used, and the effect is much the same as that outlined above, in that reducing the field will inevitably reduce the margin. As with eliminating the favourite, there will be occasions when it goes wrong, but as long as the analysis of the effect of the draw is correct, then the bias will ensure value.

This method doesn't always produce a bet as I regularly find that I can't produce a decent case for any of the runners considered, even allowing for their advantageous draw. The key here is to avoid the trap of then looking for a bet from the other runners - a badly drawn horse can never be a value bet no matter how good its form.

Another technique for reducing the field, which can be useful in major races is to employ statistics for trends established over the years in past results. A simple example of this would be to eliminate any horse out of the long handicap when considering the Grand National, since history shows that in recent years these horses have only once produced the winner.

The public prejudice

The general betting public - the mugs - place a simple and rather touching faith in the powers of the trainers and jockeys who lead the statistical success tables. I'll wager that every racegoer has overheard a comment along the lines of 'he wouldn't have sent it all this way if it wasn't any good', when two mugs are discussing the chances of a Henry Cecil-trained runner at Bath or Chepstow.

I take the view that the reverse is more likely to be true - i.e. he wouldn't be sending the horse to a minor track 200 miles from home if it had any hope of winning at Newmarket. But almost regardless of the form book, the mugs will back the Cecil nag. Knowing this, the bookmakers will make it favourite.

But what about the other side of the coin - the proven horse trained by the small trainer, and ridden by the jobbing jockey? Here is the serious punter's opportunity to obtain some value. Just as the mugs assume that anything trained by Cecil must be a good thing, so they will ignore anything trained by Smith or Jones. There are two ways in which value can be obtained from exploiting this common public prejudice.

The first is by backing horses with good form from small stables when they take on the well known names. The logic is simple - the small man needs winners to make his name and to retain his owners. He won't send a horse to Ascot or Newmarket if it's likely to be an embarrassment.

The second is to follow the fortunes of first and second season trainers who show signs of being able to do the job, and who will similarly be very keen to produce winners anywhere they can to provide the necessary publicity.

A prime example of both these categories combined can be seen in the careers of Mrs Sue Bramall and Antonin. Prior to his win in the

Ladbroke Gold Cup on New Year's Day, 1994 at Newbury, Antonin had shown form at three Grade 1 jumping tracks (Ascot, Punchestown and Wetherby), whereas the best-backed runners (Midnight Caller and Do Be Brief) had been confined to the likes of Towcester and Worcester. If Antonin had been trained by Martin Pipe or David Nicholson, or ridden by Dunwoody or Maguire, would it have started 25-1?

54 . Against The Crowd

Chapter Eight

The draw

Most punters would accept that the draw for stall positions has some bearing on the result of certain Flat races. The benefits of a particular draw in sprint races on certain tracks, such as Lingfield and Thirsk, have been widely publicised in the trade press. I don't propose to write about these sort of races in any detail, except to provide two warnings.

Firstly, it is essential always to remember that the effect of the draw is a variable. For many years in the eighties it was possible to predict the outcome of races on the straight course at Kempton with some certainty, especially when the stalls were positioned on the far rail. Standard reference books still report this bias as gospel - *Timeform* state:

"When the stalls are placed on the far side, a high draw is an enormous advantage nowadays whatever the going."

In my view this is no longer supported by the results, and hasn't been the case for the past two or three seasons. During 1993, only one winner on the straight course came from the three highest draws in ten races with the stalls on the far side. I've no idea what physical cause resulted in the bias originally (inconsistent watering is the commonest cause), but whatever it was I suspect the course managers have taken steps to eliminate the problem. The moral is that it is recent results that matter, not statistics averaged over a period of five or ten years.

Looking at the other side of the coin, let's consider the *Timeform* view of Ripon:

"On the straight course the draw is of no advantage."

And yet, in 16 races over five and six furlongs at the last six meetings in 1993, four winners came from stall one, three winners each from stalls two and three, and two winners from stall four. Of the other four, one was 4-9 favourite and another was drawn 23 of 23 in a six-furlong handicap. Simply reversing stalls one and two in a forecast would have provided three wins as follows:

| Ev bt 20-1 | 7-1 bt 8-1 | 12-1 bt 16-1 |

It can be argued that the sample is too small to be of statistical importance. I would argue that by Aug 31, anybody watching the pattern of results at Ripon over that six-week period would be well aware that 12-1 and 16-1 represented an excellent value opportunity in a five-furlong nursery handicap.

The second important factor in this type of situation is that of value. Where the bias in favour of a particular draw is widely known, it is likely that the prices on offer will be reduced to reflect the fact. High drawn horses in sprints at Lingfield and Thirsk now frequently start favourite, even when form and logic says they shouldn't. And of course they are still winning proportionately more races than you would expect, but can no longer provide profits from blindly following them.

So the advice in sprint races is to watch for short-term variations in the results and to look for situations that you can capitalise on, before the racing press have cottoned on to what is happening. In particular, look to benefit from watching races on the opening day of two-or three-day meetings and betting that the same patterns will apply on later days.

In races over trips of one mile or farther, I guess most people would seriously doubt that the draw has much effect. I hope I can demonstrate this belief is misplaced. For example, I doubt if even regular and experienced punters would believe me if I told them that the Ebor Handicap over one-and-three-quarter miles is greatly influenced by the draw - but the facts speak for themselves.

The results of the last seven runnings are as follows:

1994	Hasten To Add (9)	Admiral's Well (19)	Solartica (8)	21 ran
1993	Sarawat (9)	Oh So Risky (6)	Dreams End (1)	21 ran
1992	Quick Ransom (1)	Brier Creek (6)	Steerforth (11)	22 ran
1991	Deposki (8)	Tidemark (14)	Roll a Dollar (2)	22 ran
1990	Further Flight (3)	Bean King (9)	Holy Zeal (5)	22 ran
1989	Sapience (5)	Bush Hill (17)	Horn Dance (3)	18 ran
1988	Kneller (12)	Raslaan (6)	Tender Type (19)	21 ran

So only one winner and five placed horses have come from the 84 runners who started from stalls ten and higher, as opposed to six winners and nine placed horses from 63 runners in the single figure stalls. And the only winner drawn high, Kneller, went on to win two Group 3 races in his next two starts after carrying just 8st 1lb at York, which suggests he could have started from the two-mile pole and still given a decent performance!

The large field seems to be a significant factor here, as the bias is not apparent in the result of the Melrose Handicap run over the same course and distance the previous day, but with a much smaller field. Of course, this knowledge doesn't provide the winner of the Ebor, but it does offer a simple and proven method of reducing the number of horses who should be considered.

Whilst considering York, it's worth mentioning that this method also seems to work pretty well in the very competitive Bradford and Bingley Handicap run over one mile the day after the Ebor, with the last five winners exiting stalls two, two, one, six and four in large fields.

Taking the example of these results from York, I have found there are other tracks where a bias appears in the results on round courses, whereas most of the reporting concentrates on straight courses. These notes are based on personal observation, as well as analysis of results in recent seasons.

Ascot

In one-and-a-half-mile races with large fields, usually three each year (the Bessborough and King George V Handicap at Royal Ascot and one on Festival day), I favour high numbers on good or fast ground. The low numbers on the outside have to move across and tend to end up running wide in Swinley Bottom. On soft ground the position is reversed as jockeys have recently taken to racing wide on the sections down to and up from Swinley Bottom, taking advantage of the tree cover on the outside of the track, which reduces the effect of rainfall.

Bath

In big fields over a mile, high numbers have to start fast to get a position before the long bend into the straight, and are also pushed wide on the turn. These races are usually very rough in the first two furlongs, which are downhill, and are best avoided for betting purposes.

Goodwood

In races over seven to nine furlongs, a high number is very much favoured, especially in a double-figure field. These horses have the inside rail on the turn for home, and although this lower turn is much easier than the upper turn used in longer races, it still seems to throw low number horses wide at a crucial point in the race.

Newbury

In races over the round mile, currently only three handicaps each season, low numbers (one to five) have a considerable advantage and have produced the winner in ten of the last 15 such races. One of the horses to overcome this bias was Penny Drops in the Rothmans Royals North South Series Semi-Final in September 1993, who won from stall 17. As she went on to win the Cambridgeshire by six lengths, this result can be understood, and highlights the potential of rating horses highly when they win from an unfavourable starting stall.

The recently-introduced nine-furlong start at Newbury shows signs of also favouring low numbers, though data is as yet insufficient to be dogmatic.

Newmarket

I have successfully used a theory about low numbers with stalls on the far side on the July course for a number of years. However, for the 1994 season the management divided the July course into two, by erecting a permanent rail down the centre of the existing straight mile. On results so far this seems to have eliminated the bias, neatly demonstrating the point that circumstances change and that the present matters much more than the past.

Salisbury

The most important factor here on the straight course is how the jockeys decide to ride. In recent years the merest hint of moisture has led them to swarm to the stands' side in search of supposedly better ground. This has often led to the sight of horses who were well drawn against the far rail floundering on the worst ground in the centre of the track, as their low drawn rivals take the stand rail. When the jockeys do come stands' side here, the winner is usually the horse who gets closest to the rail, as the best strip is only a foot or two across and is hard up against the rail - this turns the races into a lottery and the only value is a bet on a low drawn John Williams' mount, as he is the only jockey who seems to have a clear idea of what is required.

Windsor

The high drawn horses in big-field mile races have a big edge, as the first three furlongs of such races are run round the bottom turn of the figure of eight, with the low drawn horses on the outside.

The basis of all these variations is that on a turning track, the wider a horse is drawn away from the rail against which the race will be run, the less its chance of establishing a good early position. If you replay a recording of any race with a big field on the tracks discussed above and stop it after about two furlongs, the horses holding the ideal positions (third, fourth, fifth, covered up and on the rail) will almost always be the ones who were well drawn. If one of the poorly drawn horses is there, run the film back and you will probably see his rider pushing hard in the first hundred yards and using up valuable energy to obtain the position.

60 . Against The Crowd

Chapter Nine

Horses to follow

I am a great believer in the merits of preparing and maintaining a list of horses to follow. From the simple fact that it involves a clear understanding of the merit, preferences and foibles of an individual horse, it enables me to spot when a horse has been given a good opportunity to win.

The size of the list is a matter of personal preference, dependent on the amount of time you have for scanning the advance entries. But the content of the list should be subject to constant scrutiny and amendment - nothing is more futile than chasing losses on a horse who has lost his form, either through injury, old age or loss of interest. The most consistent losers in any racecourse crowd or betting shop are those who back 'good old so-and-so' because he won money for them in a big race sometime back in nineteen hundred and freezing to death.

A list of horses to follow should contain only those horses who are still (one hopes) on the way up the handicap, not those who, for example, won the Cesarewitch three years ago and are now spending their declining years humping ten stones around lesser tracks.

It is much easier, and in my experience more profitable, to produce and maintain such a list for NH horses, than it is on the Flat. The modern NH programme offers a young, sound and successful horse five stages through which it can progress, as follows:

Season 1	National Hunt Flat Races (Bumpers)
Season 2	Novice Hurdles and/or Novice Handicaps
Season 3	Handicap and/or Pattern Hurdles
Season 4	Novice Chases and/or Novice Handicaps
Season 5	Handicap and/or Pattern Chases

Not many horses would go through all five of these stages in such a neat and tidy progression, but certainly in NH racing you will never encounter a situation such as that of Commander-in-Chief, who went from a debut maiden race win to a Derby win in the space of six weeks!

My method of producing a list of horses to follow over the jumps is to look for horses who are likely to move successfully from one step on the ladder to the next. In general these will be horses I have seen in action, and whose appearance as well as their form suggests a likelihood of improvement, and who fit the profile described in Chapter Two 'The Right Type'. With very rare exceptions they will be horses who are eight years old or younger, since older horses are likely to be losing their speed and/or their enthusiasm. The exceptions are likely to be long distance chasers aimed at races over three and a half miles plus, where stamina is more important than speed.

My full list of NH Horses to Follow for the 1994/5 season (written for the benefit of friends as well as myself) is included as Appendix 3, and should demonstrate the methods used in selecting horses.

On the Flat the process is a more immediate and a more fluid one, involving mainly horses I expect to go on and win in handicap company, based on the identification of the power horses as described in the earlier chapter 'The Right Type'. My own preference for staying races influences my choices, and in my view provides a more likely area for profit from this method. This is because I hope to identify horses who are improving as the distance over which they race is increased.

Successful and improving sprinters do come along (Lochsong, Glencroft, Soba), but they tend to be much easier to identify in hindsight than in real time!

One other technique on the Flat is to spot a particular race as being excellent form and to follow all the leading horses from that race. A perfect example of this came in the Bunty Scrope Maiden Stakes over one mile at Newmarket on 22 May 1993. The first six home in a field of 14 were as follows:

1	Show Faith	9-0	Hannon	10-3	
2	Lyphards Delta	8-9	Cecil	11-8 F	1½l
3	Jura Forest	9-0	Fanshawe	25-1	2l
4	Kassbaan	9-0	Scott	12-1	2l
5	Livonian	9-0	Gosden	20-1	1l
6	Learmont	9-0	Gosden	10-1	5l

Three things about this race caught my eye:

A) All six of these horses were, in the paddock, good looking horses with scope for improvement and they all moved well on the way to post.

B) All six were trained by top class trainers with a record of improving horses when they move from maiden to handicap company.

C) The race was competitive, with four of the first six home having led or disputed the lead during the final half-mile - this is very unusual in a maiden race.

Looking at the next three runs for each of these horses, we find that Show Faith won the Britannia Handicap at Royal Ascot at 6-1, Lyphards Delta won a maiden at Salisbury and a conditions race at Warwick, both at odds-on, and then a handicap at the Newmarket July meeting at 7-1.

Jura Forest was a beaten favourite in a maiden at Beverley, where he failed to handle the bend but, back on a straight course, he then won a mile handicap at Newmarket at 8-1. Kassbaan, who had led one and a half furlongs out at Newmarket, next time out won a seven-furlong handicap at Sandown at 4-1, before being unplaced behind Show Faith and Jura Forest in his next two runs.

Learmont finished fourth in another mile maiden at Kempton when unfancied, then won a one-and-a-quarter-mile maiden at Sandown at 13-8 favourite, before taking the King George V handicap at Royal Ascot over 12 furlongs at 14-1. And finally Livonian, who was off course for some time and presumably wasn't easy to train, ran seventh from a difficult draw in a mile handicap at Windsor, and then won a nine-furlong maiden at Ripon at 11-8.

Looking beyond the three runs, Lyphards Delta went on to win the Group 2 Nassau Stakes at 10-1, Kassbaan won two handicaps at Newmarket (7-2) and Sandown (9-1), and Show Faith was just touched off in the Golden Mile at Goodwood. In total these six horses produced 12 wins from 34 starts following the Newmarket maiden, producing approximate 44 points level-stake profit.

Once again the benefit of 20/20 hindsight makes this look very easy, and I freely confess that I didn't profit from all the opportunities listed above. But I did get on enough of the winners and follow the form closely enough to realise pretty quickly that the Newmarket race was a goldmine. Races that produce this sort of effect will almost always be three-year-old maiden races run at a major track before Royal Ascot, and the horses are often benefiting from an overall undervaluation of the form by the official handicapper. In other words if one is well handicapped, it is likely that the others will be similarly well in.

On the other side of the coin, it is also worth keeping a list of horses to avoid and oppose. As we've seen elsewhere it is the races with short-priced losers that are a key to finding decent value winners and I find it helps to have horses in mind as likely to fit this pattern in future races. Of course I'm not always accurate in these selections, as can be seen by my inclusion of Barton Bank and Viking Flagship in my list of horses to oppose for the 93/94 NH season! I didn't think either horse was a good enough jumper to figure in championship races, and neither did I expect David Nicholson to be able to repeat his phenomenal rate of success from the previous season.

On the Flat, horses to oppose will normally be lightly-raced animals from leading stables who have shown unsatisfactory signs in their races, who appear to lack scope for improvement based on their physical appearance, or who are likely to be raced over inappropriate distances. You might think that top trainers would learn from history, but every year good sprinters are wasted in mile races, and good milers are raced at ten and 12 furlongs.

A prime example of these methods came in the 1993 Eclipse, where the 5-2 favourite Barathea had no chance of staying the trip, and the 11-4 second favourite, Tenby, appeared not to have grown an inch since his two-year-old days - a decent bet on the proven Opera House at 5-1 was rewarded. Quite how Tenby came to start such a short-priced favourite for the Derby is an object lesson in the effects of hyperbole. The Eclipse was the first time I saw him in the flesh as a three-year-old, and I couldn't believe that such a small horse had ever been considered likely to win a Classic. The old maxim that a good little 'un can beat a good big 'un should be dismissed along with most of the other romantic garbage churned out by Mill Reef's greatest fan - it might be true once a decade, but it ain't a 4-5 shot.

Chapter Ten

Trainers and jockeys

Trainers

I place little importance in the trainer tables beloved of some punters. For example, the knowledge that Jeff King has a good record in handicaps at Bath is rendered useless when further research reveals that all the wins were achieved by one horse - Chucklestone. The information that Jack Berry has trained six winners in the last week is of little value unless you also know that all six were in two-year-old claimers and sellers and five of them started odds-on. In other words to benefit from following trainer statistics you have to dig a little deeper than the bare figures to get at the truth.

I concern myself only with the current form of a stable, whilst taking into account that factors like those mentioned above may twist the figures. And I generally place more importance in watching for stables that are out of form, rather than those reported as being in good form. The spells of good form are often over by the time the statistics are able to reflect them, but stables out of form often suffer for a whole season as illness affects all the horses.

The tables published in the daily racing press show quite clearly which stables are in form and which are struggling, but despite the ready availability of this information, punters will still support horses from yards that haven't saddled a winner for weeks.

One significant factor to note is that the best horses in a stable will often buck the trend and overcome the problems - for example Zeta's Lad managed to win a major race at Haydock over jumps in early 1994, even though the John Upson yard was stricken with a virus - it is the middle range and moderate horses who cannot cope. Equally, a long losing spell will often be ended by a class horse with the effect of returning the stable to form as confidence returns. A prime example of this would be the win by Arctic Kinsman for Nigel Twiston-Davies in the opening race of the 1994 Cheltenham Festival after three weeks without a winner.

It is also worth repeating the advice given in Chapter Seven, that if the horse is good enough then so is the trainer. The star horse in a small stable will be given star treatment and will sometimes reflect that on the racecourse. If the form the horse has shown for this trainer is what leads you to fancy it, then don't be put off by the Cecil or Pipe runner in the same race. The list of successes from small stables, especially in jumping, is endless - at the Cheltenham Festival alone in recent years I can offer Nortons Coin, Flakey Dove, Danoli, Repeat The Dose, and who had heard of Martin Pipe when he saddled Baron Blakeney to win the Triumph Hurdle?

Many serious punters swear by the benefits of following a specific stable or stables, getting to know their methods and patterns. In my view this is little different to my own preference for following horses. In both cases it is the edge that is obtained over the mass of punters that makes the system successful. It is only my own experience as an owner that deters me from adopting the stable method, as I found that I started seeing the horses through rose coloured spectacles, instead of judging them impartially as I would other horses.

Jockeys

I'm surely not alone in being irritated by the mindless praise doled out to winning jockeys by the likes of Francome, Lindley, Oaksey and Pitman, when the simple task of steering the best horse to victory is described as a 'great ride', whilst the efforts of those in behind on inferior horses are ignored. The irrepressible Richard Fox wrote recently of one such ride, when he won a staying handicap by a short head and was widely lauded for his timing - he freely admitted that he had made a complete mess of it and that getting up close home was entirely due to the ability of the horse, who, properly ridden, would have won by several lengths.

To listen to the TV pundits with their zero criticism style, you would think we are blessed with the best collection of jockeys in the history of racing. That is not a view I share!

On the Flat we currently have very few stars, a body of 20 to 30 competent riders and not much else. Dettori and Weaver are clearly the coming men and both seem to have the priceless gift of being in the right place through a race. Of the others, only the presence of

John Williams would ever persuade me to back one horse on my short list rather than another.

Over the jumps the position is similar with Dunwoody and Maguire streets ahead of the opposition, but the competent list is much smaller, and my personal list of incompetents (whose rides I won't back regardless of their form) is headed by one who is referred to in my circle of racegoing friends as 'The Ten Pound Penalty'.

Overall I don't attach too much importance to trainers and jockeys as far as punting is concerned. They rate below such considerations as the horse's form, going and distance preferences, class and handicap mark, draw and/or jumping ability. But a serious punter should certainly hold opinions on the ability of trainers and jockeys, and act accordingly.

Chapter Eleven

The sand

In common with most regular racegoers, when all-weather racing was first introduced to this country, I was pretty dismissive. It seemed to cater entirely for poor quality horses, often in uncompetitive races, with a sparse crowd ensuring a weak betting market.

My first, and so far only visit to Lingfield to watch sand racing did little to alter that view. The track is so far from the stands that the racing seems remote, and the layout of the course seems to accentuate the American hell-for-leather nature of the racing.

Two recent events have changed my views. The first was the realisation that in the event of a prolonged freeze during the winter, my activities would come to a complete halt. Looking back at betting records from the years prior to my conversion to full-time punting showed that a barren month was not uncommon.

The second event was the opening of the new all-weather track at Wolverhampton. My first tentative visit on a Monday afternoon in January, 1994 made me an instant convert. The whole place is an eye-opener to regulars who are used to spending their winter afternoons partaking of the delights(?) of Towcester or Worcester. To begin with the car parks are all tarmac, with marked parking spaces, the entry fee to Tatts is a flat £6, and the stands provide an excellent view of the action. The members and the hospitality shower are shoved well out of harm's way in a tiny enclosure down beyond the winning post and in winter weather can be relied upon to remain in their hutch.

The track itself is no more than an oval Chester, but all the action takes place close to the customer, and even modest horses produce dramatic racing. With a safety limit of 13, and small fields an exception, most of the races had an ideal shape for form analysis and betting. And best of all, the form worked out consistently - with a small pool of horses competing regularly, and with no fluctuations in the going, and with the help of one more discovery, I found that I could spot value bets with ease.

The extra discovery, though, was the key - the realisation that in races over distances from five to nine furlongs, the horses drawn in stalls one to four might as well have stayed at home for all the chance they had of winning. Other professionals and journalists have spotted this enormous bias and reported it in the trade press, but predictably this essential information is freely ignored by bookmakers and punters alike.

Jockeys have clearly worked out that the inside rail is death, and almost all now make for the centre of the course in the home straight. But the results still show the same bias, which leads me to conclude that the damage to the low drawn horses is done in the early stages of the races when they are forced to race close to the inside fence. My own theory as to the cause of this bias, lies in the rolling of the track which is carried out between races and presumably between meetings.

Two tractors towing rollers are used, one against the inside fence, and one against the outside fence. But as the rollers are more than half track wide, there is a strip in the centre of the track which is double rolled every time the equipment is used. This firmer strip lines up with starting stalls six, seven and eight in every race, and it is these stalls that produce the most winners. The same equipment is used at Southwell, but the track there is wider - 16 starting stalls as opposed to 13 at Wolverhampton.

From the first 16 races run at Wolverhampton over the seven-furlong, eight-furlong and nine-furlong trips, all of which had at least ten runners, half were won by the horse drawn seven. The level-stake profit was enormous. Since the winter season at Wolverhampton ended, the results from the subsequent fortnightly Saturday evening meetings haven't shown the same bias. This may be due to the new track settling down, it may be due to maintenance work, or it may simply be a result of the warmer weather affecting the material substance of the track. However, when the next winter season starts I'll be watching the pattern of results and hoping that a bias can be found.

One other factor that needs watching at Wolverhampton is the marked decline in SP percentages that has occurred since the early meetings. Small crowds and opening shows with 40 per cent margins for the bookies will deter serious punters, leading to a Catch 22 situation.

A visit to Wolverhampton is recommended to all punters - it may not be as aesthetically pleasing as Goodwood or Cheltenham, but it is the future, and for serious punters it is excellent news, so long as the market remains strong.

72 . Against The Crowd

Chapter Twelve

The Tote

As presently set up in this country, the Tote is almost completely useless as a betting medium. If we had a Tote monopoly I would still expect to show a profit on my betting, assuming that the percentage extracted by the Tote was reasonable. After all, in a Tote system, it becomes even clearer that winning punters are dependent on the existence of losing punters.

The proviso on the Tote percentage is a vital one, and one that is rarely discussed in this country. At present their take is 16 per cent from the win pool, which is acceptable, but substantially more from all other pools, which is not. The problem is that their costs are fixed, but their pool sizes are small - the take has to be a large percentage in order to meet their expenses.

So are there any opportunities for a professional to benefit from the existence of a Tote system in parallel with the bookies? The answer is yes, but only on a very small number of days each year.

Firstly let's dismiss those Tote bets that should be completely ignored:

Place Only - absolutely no value and always tiny pools, so that any half decent bet will destroy the odds. Anyway, why do you think it will be placed, but not win?

Dual Forecast - the Tote often boasts about what good value this bet is compared with the bookies' alternatives. In actual fact it's a rotten value bet and the dividends quoted in the adverts only arose because nobody backed them for more than a quid. In my experience a £5 dual forecast bet will at least halve the displayed return if it was over £40.

Placepot - only mug punters of the highest order would be interested in this stupid bet and the fact that it is so popular is a great relief. I shared a table at Doncaster last year with a family group before racing. They'd won on the Placepot the day before and were still arguing about it. As my *Sporting Life* and binoculars marked me as an expert, I was asked to explain. They had invested £16 in a perm and were very excited when they got a 20-1 shot placed in one race and got through to the sixth still alive, convinced they were going to win hundreds. After a 20-minute wait after the last, they collected £6.20. The 20-1 shot had been placed along with a 4-5 favourite and a 3-1 second favourite, and all the other results were equally predictable. When I left to go to the parade ring A (father) and B (wife) were still convinced that C (son/husband, poor chap), had filled it in wrongly and cheated them out of a fortune!

The problem with the placepot is thus clearly demonstrated - the dividend is highly variable, dependent on horses other than the ones you have supported. In addition, the takeout at 29 per cent is a killer to any hope of value, and there is never any money carried forward to help offset this deduction. And even with the recent take-up of the Tote Direct terminals, the pools are still not big enough to take a professional sized bet without markedly reducing the dividend if successful.

So we are left with the Win and the Jackpot. Both can, on rare occasions, offer some value.

Tote Win

When the pool is big enough to take a £100 bet on an outsider without drastically reducing the payout, there is a system which can be employed profitably. At present this only happens when the win pool on a race exceeds £20,000, which in my experience will only happen at the major racing Festivals. The system can only be operated on course, where the current dividends and the size of the pool are displayed on the Tote screens.

The mathematics are straightforward - if there is a pool of £20K after deductions (i.e. £24K in the pool), then it takes £500 in stakes to produce a dividend of £40. If you bet an additional £100 on the same horse, increasing the stake to £600, the dividend will drop to £33.30. Of course, the pattern of betting after your bet, up to the off may push the dividend further down, or back up again. This highlights the essential problem of Tote betting - the uncertain return.

I've used the system at the major Festival meetings as follows. The race should have a large field, where the Tote take of 16 per cent is likely to be considerably less than the percentage profit contained in the bookies' over-round, or margin, which can go as high as 40-50 per cent in big handicaps. It should also be a race where you are not committed to a specific selection, but are happy to produce a short list of possibles. It can be especially effective in races where you think the draw could have an effect on the result. Once the win pool reaches £10,000 compare the dividends on screen for your short-listed horses with the early morning and current ring prices. Where the Tote dividend is substantially higher, you have the opportunity for a value bet.

Delay placing your bet as long as possible - if someone else is pursuing the same idea on the same horse the value may disappear - and use the formula outlined above to measure the likely impact of your bet to ensure that you won't be removing the differential that provides the value. In fact you'll find that on some outsiders the Tote dividend will offer two or three times more than the equivalent return from the bookies.

My best win using this idea came in the Ebor at York in 1993. My form book fancy was Night Clubbing, trained by Reg Akehurst, who also had Sarawat in the race, which had been well backed antepost. But I didn't feel strongly enough about the race (and I hadn't at that stage spotted the draw bias) to go for a proper bet. The bookies' best offers were 14-1 for Sarawat and 33-1 for Night Clubbing, but the Tote returns with over £20K in the pool were 36-1 for Sarawat and 77-1 for Night Clubbing. Unwilling to oppose the apparent stable fancy, I bet £100 win on each - Sarawat won and returned a dividend of £33.80.

Other winners which highlight the potential of this system have been Barton Bank at Aintree (Tote £45.10, SP 20-1) and Master Planner at York (Tote £26.60, SP 16-1). Another example of the startling value that can occur was demonstrated by a bet I had at the 1994 Cheltenham Festival, where the win pool regularly exceeds £100,000 for each race. I had backed Captain Dolford for the long distance handicap hurdle, taking 16-1 antepost and again on the day with a rails bookie. When I checked the Tote screen ten minutes before the off, I was amazed to discover that the dividend was over £75, with more than £60,000 already in the pool. A bet of £200 had so little effect that I went in again for the same, and even that left the dividend around £44 just before the off. The S.P. for this horse was 14-1 - sadly for the story it ran like the 75-1 shot that other Tote punters had decreed!

So in addition to the system described above, if you're having a proper bet in the ring at one of the Festivals, if time permits, it's worthwhile checking the Tote screens and having a top-up if the value is available.

Tote Jackpot

A potentially huge profit-maker for the Tote, and hence a boost for racing, the Jackpot is a dismal failure 99 per cent of the time. As a result of the Tote's reluctance to salt the Jackpot pools with sufficient cash to attract the punters, the pools remain small and unattractive. A classic Catch 22. Indeed, at a recent Wolverhampton all-weather meeting on a Monday afternoon, the Jackpot paid under £2,000 to a £1 stake on a day when a £1 SP accumulator would have paid over £4,400! As to why the Jackpot was on offer at Wolverhampton on a Monday in February, only the Tote knows the answer.

Even worse, on Magnet Cup day at York in 1994, a Jackpot with no carry forward paid £441 to a £1 stake on a day when five favourites and a second-favourite obliged. A £1 accumulator at SP on the same six horses would have paid over £3,000. Quite incredibly there was no riot at York, and no comment in the trade press or the letters columns about this travesty.

From our point of view, the only time to get involved is when the pool has a substantial carry forward, in order to offset the 29 per cent Tote rake-off before the dividends are calculated and to provide a sufficient pool to guard against the circumstance described above. My own preference is a carry forward of at least six figures, to a card where I can spot two banker bets, which can be mixed with multiple selections in other races to produce a permutation with a chance. Your selection shouldn't include all six favourites, nor should it include rank outsiders. Whatever level of stake you use, I feel that your perm should have only about one line for every £1,000 carried forward.

Keep the stakes reasonable, because realistically this is money you have to write off - the win will be great, but like the football pools it will also be rare. It is easy to be sucked into mistaken thinking on the Jackpot, as this example quoted to me by a Tote official demonstrates. Following the Cheltenham Festival in 1993, there was a carry over of £110,000 to Lingfield on Friday. One credit punter invested £2,800 in a perm of 28,000 lines at 10p each. Had he included the day's six winners he would have collected under £4,000 after tax - the equivalent of putting £2,800 on a 1-2 favourite off course! In fact he fell at the second hurdle! Had the six favourites won, he would have won the Jackpot and lost over £2,000 on the day.

Doubtless this would have impressed his mates in the pub rather more than his bank manager.

78 . Against The Crowd

Chapter Thirteen

Money

As the object of the entire exercise, it could be argued that this chapter is placed too late in the book. But the positioning is deliberate, so that the other basics are established as the framework against which we can discuss the financial considerations.

Like all punters, I started out as a low-stake bettor, using a percentage of my pocket money for my first ever wager of 2s 6d (12½p) each-way. As the years passed and my confidence grew in line with my financial resources, so my average stake increased, until it's now over £300.

Assuming that you are able to operate from a capital base, rather than betting from income, there are three considerations which should dictate your staking:

A   What are your profit expectations?
B   How many bets will you have?
C   How many losers can you afford?

Let me give you my answers to these questions to demonstrate the calculation. My aspiration is to make an annual profit of at least £10,000 - not a great sum, but a fair income when you remember it is tax free and that investment income should help to cover my racing expenses. To achieve this profit, I recognise that I must plan to turn over approximately £100,000 in bets, since a ten per cent profit on turnover is what I can reasonably expect, based on my records for the past ten years.

As I now attend 150 meetings in an average year, a figure of 300 bets is acceptable - more would mean stretching the rules we discussed earlier. Indeed fewer bets might be desirable.

Clearly, on these figures my average stake must be £333 and that figure was almost exactly matched in 1993 when I had 291 bets. If I could reduce my number of bets, then the average stake would have to increase. But I feel comfortable at the current level, and at anything over £500 I start to suffer doubts that get in the way of my normal analysis of a race. Higher stakes also mean bigger losses when the inevitable losing run comes along, making confidence and 'bottle' harder to maintain. In essence I'm operating in my own comfort zone, and I recognise that my results are likely to be better if I stick to that.

For me the issue of stop-loss doesn't arise, since my capital base can sustain me through any credible losing run. I would have given up the game in despair well before my money ran out! But for the average punter the stop-loss question is paramount - even if your answers to questions one and two dictate a £300 average stake, that isn't practical if your capital is under £10,000. So the questions of profit and turnover have to be subordinated to the practical limits imposed by your capital base.

Other text books offer advice that your standard bet should be five per cent or even ten per cent of your capital. If you win, your staking increases, but if you lose your staking falls. These sort of methods might operate well for those who are backing favourites (good luck to them and thank the Lord for their existence), but if you are backing 6-1 shots and start with five losers, having a smaller stake on the eventual winner than you had on any of the losers is going to do nothing for your confidence or your prospects of making an overall profit.

My personal method is to operate mainly in a narrow band either side of my desired average. In practice I stick to a minimum stake of £250 and a normal maximum of £400, which produces the right sort of total turnover for me. I can and do exceed the maximum if circumstances are right, but these occasions are entirely to do with 'feel' and confidence, rather than any plan that could be defined on paper. The minimum is a useful marker when considering a bet using the rule - 'If it isn't worth a minimum bet, then it isn't worth a bet at all'

This avoids the sort of thinking that leads to a small bet 'just in case', or simply to have an interest in an otherwise dull race. These quickly add up to a substantial dent in your profits as properly kept records will show, and when one of them does win you simply wish you'd had a proper bet.

So overall the recommendation is to decide on an average with which you feel comfortable, and which fits in with your capital resources, and then set a minimum just below that average and stick to it.

The crucial result of this staking method is that we have a similar level of stake on a 10-1 shot as on a 2-1 shot, which emphasises the benefit of beating the price at longer odds as discussed in Chapter Six 'The Market'. As long as discipline is maintained, then the common trap of the big bet on the short-priced horse and vice versa is avoided.

In the earlier chapter on 'The Four C's', I mooted the need for a capital base of five times the expected annual profit. I can now confess that that was designed to scare off any reader who was reading this in the hope or expectation of making a full time living from betting. Clearly it can be done with a lower starting level than that, but I do feel that much depends on the psychology of the punter.

Personally, having only taken the plunge full time when my capital was already more than sufficient, I can only guess how I would have handled a smaller pot. But I can remember how it felt back in the days when I was betting from income, and I knew that my next bet either had to be a winner, or my last bet until next payday. If I had that feeling now, I know for certain that it would influence my thinking, with the likely effect of making winners at any price appear preferable to winners at a value price.

I feel this is the key to money management for the punter - that the punter MUST manage the money, not the money manage the punter. In other words, the placing of a bet and the amount of the stake must be decisions taken in isolation and not based on the results of previous bets. In my days as an amateur I often went for a big win in the last race of the day if I was in front, hoping for a really big profit on the day in proportion to my stake, but happy to go home even if the last one got beat. But far worse were the times I chased losses by having hopeful, poorly researched bets, in dreadfully complicated races, with the staking decided by how much cash I had left in my wallet! If you encounter this problem yourself, try asking a simple question before you place a bet: 'Would I be having this bet if I were in front on the day?'

Perhaps the hardest part of the adjustment from mug to professional punter is facing up to the fact that there will be more losers than winners, more losing days than winning days, more losing weeks etc... It is essential that losing bets are recorded, analysed, and then put into perspective and not allowed to over-influence future thinking.

Chapter Fourteen

Betting diary

This diary details the bets I made at the major meetings during 1994, totalling 24 racing days and covering both NH and Flat racing. Although it is written with the benefit of hindsight, I have attempted to relate honestly the reasons for placing each bet and my reactions to the results. The number of mistakes uncovered in the following pages will confirm that even authors with good ideas on paper can be diverted by the excitement of the chase. But most of the bets should help to show how the methods discussed in the earlier chapters are applied in practice.

Each bet is logged exactly as it appears in my own records. The odd amounts that sometimes appear in the stake and return columns reflect my practice of spreading my bets around in the ring, so that not all the money is always invested at the same price.

Saturday February 26   Kempton

Including this one day meeting might be regarded as cheating in order to get the diary off to a winning start, but it was also a day that provided plenty of useful pointers, in more ways than one.

ANTONIN

| 3m H'cap Chase | £3,750-520 | SP 7-1 |

I had backed Antonin when he won at 25-1 at Newbury on January 1, so not surprisingly I felt considerable affection for him. I'm usually wary of backing a horse just because of a previous win, but he fitted the profile of a young, improving horse from a small stable with a light weight, thanks to the presence of The Fellow. As the only six-year-old against just three eight-year-olds and 12 older horses his price looked good value. His win was achieved in remarkable style, leading five out and then dropping away on the home turn before bursting through at the last to run away with the race - a perfect example of the pace young horses can produce against older rivals.

GLENBROOK D'OR

3¹/₂m H'cap Chase   **£8,000-290**   **SP 25-1**

This horse was high on my list of horses to follow as a sure winner of a long distance handicap chase. Last time out he had led at the last, but been caught in the final stride, over three miles, five furlongs at Warwick. Although he was 17lb out of the handicap here I still gave him a fair chance. The handicapping for long distance races tends to be based on form a horse has shown at shorter trips and being out of the handicap doesn't stop a horse with genuine stamina from running well. The performance of Just So in the Grand National was a prime example. I managed three bets of £1,000-30 and five of £1,000-40. The horse was last but beginning to close up when falling seven fences out, but wouldn't have beaten Master Oats.

This sort of bet might be regarded as a waste of money, but Antonin was 25-1 when he won at Newbury and would have looked just as daft on paper if he hadn't won. One success with this sort of bet can do wonders for your profit and your confidence. Glenbrook D'or repaid my support later with a 10-1 win in the Midland Grand National over four and a quarter miles at Uttoxeter.

This single day at Kempton produced EIGHT winners at the Cheltenham Festival and despite watching all these races, I didn't back any of them at Cheltenham. A useful reminder that even when you are betting, you should always be thinking ahead, asking yourself what you've seen and what was the value of the form.

Tuesday March 15   Cheltenham

I had attended only one meeting the previous week and had put in plenty of work with the formbook and the video in preparation for the Festival. This meeting provides a number of problems for a professional, apart from the difficulty of the racing. The size of the crowd makes it impossible to carry out the usual rituals of visiting the pre-parade ring, the paddock, and the betting ring, prior to watching the race. I use a reserved seat in the main stand to ensure that I can see all the races comfortably, and make more use of my Tote credit account than normal, as well as betting on the rails in cash.

BAYDON STAR

2m Novice Chase	Ante-post £1,400-350	SP 5-2
	Ante-post £1,500-500	

I backed him ante-post at 4-1 five days in advance (on-course at Towcester), confident that Coonawara would by-pass the race. On the day, even with that rival present, I still thought him the class act of the race and my banker for the meeting. His defeat by Nakir was disappointing, but the bet still looks valid. Every so often you'll be beaten by a horse when it first reveals its true ability. Nakir's subsequent form confirms him as a better two-miler than Baydon Star.

USHERS ISLAND

3¹/₄m H'cap Chase	£2,700-600	SP 9-2

This looked a weak renewal of the Ritz Club Chase, with Antonin an obvious favourite after his Kempton win. I deserted him for three reasons; the ground was faster than at Kempton and Newbury, the undulating track, which he had never raced over before, and the 11st 10lb he had to carry. I had seen Ushers Island jump brilliantly to win on good ground at Wetherby the previous autumn and he had won over four miles here, as had recent winners of this race Bigsun and Seagram, both of whom I backed.

I think the only thing wrong with this bet was the price, which didn't offer enough value to cover the poor recent form of the stable. Ushers Island was never at the races as Antonin overcame some poor jumping on the first circuit to win easily. Six weeks later Ushers Island won the Whitbread Gold Cup at 20-1, with Antonin in second. Coming up with the right answers isn't the only requirement in this game - you also have to know on which day the question is being asked!

CAPTAIN DOLFORD

3¹/₄m H'cap Hurdle	£10,000-600	SP 14-1
	Ante-Post £ 4,800-300	
	Tote Win £ 400	

To say that I got carried away with this bet would be gross understatement. Of course if the horse had won, the tale would have been told in great detail in Chapter One. As it is, part of the story has already been told in the piece on using the Tote Win pool as a source of value.

I had been on Captain Dolford twice at 11-2 when he won at Newbury and Chepstow in mid-winter. I had avoided him when he was beaten in the qualifier for this race at Nottingham (trip too short) and when he slipped up in a small field at Ascot (price too short). My conviction that Captain Dolford would be back next year to win the Stayers Hurdle had been voiced abroad, and I regarded this as merely a stepping stone along the way.

In the midst of all this euphoria, I had conveniently excused myself from studying the form of his 31 rivals. I had also ignored the fact that both his wins had come on heavy ground and that both had involved front running in smaller fields. When Victor Chandler was alone in offering 16-1 on the morning of the race, the only decision left was how much to take off him. My pre-racing request for £10,000 to £600 was accepted on the nod by the great man himself and I proudly showed the slip to my friends. Betting with Victor was surely evidence of my growing professional status.

With the value-seeking Tote bets placed later, I stood to net over £30,000 on this race. The result was in fact exactly what I deserved and my various slips and tickets were worthless with over a circuit to run.

Over dinner that evening I reflected on a £2,750 loss on the day and later got out my set of betting rules for the season to provide some salutary bedtime reading.

Wednesday March 16   Cheltenham

TRAVADO
2m Pattern Chase   **£400 Tote Win**

I rated the horse as a likely winner, but hadn't expected to make a bet at the price in a competitive race. He had the advantage of youth over Remittance Man, and Viking Flagship lacked previous experience at Cheltenham, but neither of those rivals could be completely dismissed. However, the Tote screens showed close to 5-1 shortly before the off, providing a decent edge over the returned price of 10-3.

MAILCOM
3m Novice Chase   **£5,600-400**   **SP 14-1**

Mailcom finished only three lengths behind the favourite One Man at Ascot in their previous race, despite jumping left at most fences. At the prices, he was the value bet to reverse that result on this stiffer left hand track. In addition his stable (Jenny Pitman) regularly produces a useful performer in this race. He was hampered at halfway when Honest Word fell, but that only increased the scale of his defeat.

FLORIDA SKY
4m Novice Chase   **£200 Tote Win**

A small bet to take advantage of a considerable Tote/SP difference about a horse I had seen jump and stay well to win over three miles, three furlongs a few weeks earlier at Taunton. The stable (John Upson) had been struggling all season and betting against that sort of trend is rarely rewarded, even if the particular horse you are backing has shown some form.

DUBLIN FLYER
2¹/₂m H'cap Chase   **£3,000-360**   **SP 7-1**

This horse fitted the pattern of a young, improving chaser with good recent form (a 20-length win at Wincanton featuring superb jumping). He ran an excellent race and saw off all the opponents I had been worried about, only to be headed by the remarkable 11-year-old Elfast who broke just about every statistical trend associated with this race.

I was really hopeful before this event and the size of the bet indicates the first ebbing of confidence brought about by my losses on the week so far. It's much easier to write that each bet is a separate entity, than to apply the principle in practice in the midst of this sort of meeting.

Thursday March 17   Cheltenham

AVRO ANSON
3m Pattern Hurdle   **£3,600-400**   **SP 8-1**

The Stayers Hurdle has been transformed as a result of being moved from Tuesday to Thursday and thus from the Old Course to the New Course. The distance has been considerably reduced, which is highlighted by the race time. This year the race was run in five minutes 48 seconds, compared with six minutes 34 seconds for Nomadic Way on the same going two years earlier. So, whereas stamina used to be the key to finding the winner, now it is speed. Hence my choice of Avro Anson, who had twice been beaten for stamina since his excellent second to Triple Witching over two and a half miles when conceding 10lbs, in what still looked the best handicap hurdle of the season.

Those who remember the race will know that I suffered the punter's worst experience of a winner who throws the race away by swerving on the run-in. There was never any doubt that Avro Anson would be disqualified in favour of Balasani, thus wiping four grand off my accounts, in addition to ending the prospects of our £200 syndicate scooping the Jackpot pool.

ONCE STUNG
3¹/₄m Hunter Chase   £3,250-500   SP 7-1

I felt that Double Silk was opposable on the basis of his form for the season so far, having achieved nothing that his main rivals here couldn't have done just as easily. Once Stung had finished third behind Double Silk last year in this race and, being two years younger, seemed to me to have a fair chance of reversing the form.

When the odds-on favourite wins easily and your bet runs poorly, this sort of wager looks dreadful with hindsight. But the logic of opposing short-priced horses with good value rivals remains sound and will produce profits in the long run. The price of Double Silk (2-5) had much more to do with hype than form.

CYPHRATE
2m H'cap Chase   £250 Tote Win

From a short list of three, which certainly didn't include the winner Snitton Lane, this was by far the best value on the Tote, at over 25-1. An excellent price for a horse who had finished second in the Champion Chase a year earlier, was trained by Martin Pipe and ridden by Charlie Swan. None of those factors helped him avoid last place!

TAROUDANT

2m H'cap Hurdle	£4,800-400	SP 14-1
	£250 Tote Win	

Taroudant finished third at Chepstow in November, when Avro Anson was second. His run at Doncaster on March 5 looked to me like a public gallop in preparation for this race. I took 12-1 with Tote Credit in the morning, which proved a misjudgement of the market. The Tote cash bet was added to take advantage of a 17-1 win price. The horse ran poorly, taking my career record in the County Hurdle to approximately 0-15.

A dispiriting week, with a total deficit of almost £6,000 to be entered into my records. Looking back the next day, my main mistake seemed to be taking early prices without waiting to see what value the Tote win pool might offer. For example the £1,300 lost on Captain Dolford could have been reduced to £400, since the return offered by the Tote bet alone would have been more than sufficient reward if the horse had won.

The week was partially rescued by an off-course bet of £3,000-300 tax paid on Glenbrook D'Or in the Midland Grand National. But even that success left me wondering whether I might have staked more if I'd gone to the meeting, or if my confidence hadn't been affected by events at the Festival.

Even professionals always wish they had bigger stakes on their winners and smaller ones on their losers!

Thursday April 7   Aintree

JAZILAH

2m Novice Hurdle	£700-400	SP 7-4

A banker bet because the main opposition, Dreams End, had made mistakes in both his recent races and I was sure that the three close hurdles in the straight would catch him out. In addition Jazilah had beaten the Cheltenham winner Arctic Kinsman easily at Kempton in his last race.

It was close, but Dreams End did make a crucial mistake at the last and Jazilah just held off the four-year-old Winter Forest.

KENTISH PIPER

2³/₄m H'cap Chase   £4,000-400   SP 7-1

This horse and I are old adversaries and he owes me a small fortune. Victor Chandler's early price offer of 10-1 seemed to offer an opportunity to square the books with both horse and bookie. I felt that the trip, course and ground would all suit. Defeat by a neck meant a losing bet, but no complaints about the effort put in by the horse or the value of the bet.

CAPABILITY BROWN

3m H'cap Chase   £2,750-340   SP 7-1

By now the ground was pretty desperate after heavy rain. In recent years it has regularly paid dividends to fall back on a Martin Pipe-trained runner under these circumstances and with at least half of the eight runners likely to be unsuited by conditions, Capability Brown looked the value. In the event he ran like a horse who was enjoying the weather even less than the punters.

Friday April 8   Aintree

You may remember that by the end of the afternoon, doubts were expressed over whether the Grand National could be run the next day due to the state of the ground. If I have ever been wetter on a racecourse, despite wearing head to toe waterproof protection all day, then I'm glad I can't remember the experience. Betting under these conditions means throwing away the form book and concentrating entirely on horses who have proven their ability to cope with heavy ground.

FORCE SEVEN

2¹/₂m Pattern Chase   £3,000-280   SP 8-1

This bet was based on the belief that the first three in the betting (Travado, Remittance Man, Deep Sensation) would all hate the conditions and would struggle even to complete the course. Left with Force Seven and Katabatic, I opted for the younger horse with the better recent form. Murphy's Law clearly ruled here as Force Seven fell at the second and Katabatic won by 20 lengths at 14-1. Only later did it occur to me that I could have backed both and still obtained a good value bet.

MONSIEUR LE CURE
3m Novice Chase   £1,250-500   SP 7-4

This horse won a novice hurdle in similar conditions at Newton Abbot by a distance, so I had no doubts about him handling the ground. With little to beat apart from those he had already dealt with at Cheltenham, 5-2 seemed excellent value. The fact that he carried a 6lb penalty for that win was rendered irrelevant by the weather. This performance made the day worthwhile despite the downpour, as the winner put in a round of jumping and galloping to warm the heart.

With this profit tucked away, I was happy to let the remaining slogging matches go by without involvement. Grand National day isn't one I attend - the crowd would make the job impossible and I usually go to Hereford.

Tuesday June 14   Royal Ascot

Royal Ascot represents the start of my main period of betting during the Flat season. Prior to this meeting I'd had five winners from just 21 bets on turf racing, ignoring the bets made during the winter at Wolverhampton.

BENEFICIAL
10f Pattern   £4,000-280   SP 14-1

Beneficial had a good winning record as a three-year-old, including success at this meeting over one and a half miles. I felt that his poor run last time at Sandown in a ten-furlong Group 3 race could be forgiven as he was drawn wide in stall one in a field of 14, and couldn't be covered up.

He looked superb in the paddock and moved fluently to post - 14-1 looked excellent value. He ran fourth in what proved to be a high class Group 2 race, with the winner and second both successful in Group 1 company later in the season.

MOON KING

6f 2-y-o Pattern   **£250 Tote Win**

I had been impressed by his debut win at Newbury and he was the best mover on the way to post. The Tote offered better value than the books. Beaten a neck into second, this is the sort of result that upsets an amateur. But it satisfies a professional who knows that if all the horses he backs run as well as the last two bets, then enough will win to produce profits.

TILTY

2½m H'cap   **£4,000-230**   **SP : 16-1**
                        £200 Tote Win

I had marked Tilty as a possible winner of this race as early as the end of the previous season, when he showed the necessary stamina by finishing second in a two-mile handicap at Ascot. He also won twice over long distances on fast ground. His preparation over shorter trips this season seemed to me to be designed to have him ready for this race. The engagement of M Kinane to ride suggested that I had read the planning correctly.

I might have made a larger bet, except that the price looked a bit skinny in a 30-runner field. Two of my five biggest-ever wins have come in this race in recent years, with Cabochon and Balasani. In the event he ran appallingly, showing clear signs of distaste for racing and trailing home in 25th place. This is the sort of bet that upsets a professional! A good deal of my journey home was spent trying to decide if I could or should have spotted previous warning signs about Tilty.

Wednesday June 15   Royal Ascot

MEHTHAAF

1m Pattern   **£1,500-300**   **SP 5-1**

I felt that Mehthaaf had the best overall form and despite the concerns expressed about her ability on fast ground, she moved to post quite freely. At double the price of Las Meninas she was clearly a value bet. In finishing third, she beat all those I had included on my short list, so no complaints.

NASHVILLE BLUES

1m Handicap   £200 Win
                               £100 Place Tote

This was another horse who I felt had been prepared specifically with Ascot in mind, having run out of her class in a conditions event at Epsom last time. Her previous second of 23 over a mile at Newbury confirmed that she could act on a straight course in a big field. I had also read a report that she was in foal, a condition which often brings about improvement in a mare who continues to race.

In this case, however, the effect seemed opposite, as she never got into the race and her form continued to decline over the next two months. Interestingly, the winner came from stall 30, as did Venture Capitalist later in the week, and Wizard King from stall 28 (of 28).

BLAAZING JOE

2m Pattern   £3,000-420   SP 5-1

With neither of the Henry Cecil-trained pair, who started first and second favourite, having convinced me that they would stay this trip, this was a must betting race. I latched on to the 7-1 in the ring about Blaazing Joe, who had won a fast-run conditions race over 14 furlongs at York on similar ground. Despite having seen the eventual winner Silver Wedge when he won over 12 furlongs at Newbury, I hadn't considered him, even as a possible outsider. So a potentially good bet which produced a disappointing result, with Blaazing Joe beaten two furlongs out.

JOHNS ACT

1½m Handicap   £3,800-400   SP 9-1

This race demonstrates one of the problems of race analysis; deciding which of several factors is the most important. As I wrote in the chapter about the draw, I prefer high numbers in these races at Ascot. But on this occasion, I couldn't make out a sufficiently good case for any of the high drawn horses to overcome my form fancy, Johns Act, who was drawn eight of 20, a position I thought he might get away with. I also misjudged the market here, missing early price offers of 12-1 about my selection.

With hindsight, I probably should have passed on the race. The winner Master Charlie was drawn 18 - his previous and subsequent form all pointed to his high draw being vital to his success. But Hasten To Add managed second from stall one, a sterling effort to overcome such a big disadvantage. He confirmed his quality with his running later in the season. Johns Act ran poorly and his subsequent form suggested he wouldn't have won this from any starting position.

This time I had rated form as more important than draw, but next season I'll take the alternative view.

After two days of Royal Ascot my seasonal profit had been reduced considerably, but I was happy with most of the bets I had made. I've never attended Gold Cup day because of the crowds and I rarely bother with Friday as the races on that day are mostly of the type I don't play. Had I spotted the bias towards a high draw on the straight course before Friday's racing, rather than much later, some value bets could have been placed.

Tuesday July 5   Newmarket

MYSELF
6f 2-y-o Pattern   **£900-400**   **SP 9-4**

For me, the Ascot run by Myself (second over five furlongs from a low draw) was considerably better than anything the opposition had achieved. She looked the part here, moved well to post, and hailed from a stable (Chapple-Hyam) with an excellent recent record in two-year-old pattern events. She didn't produce the power I'd anticipated in finishing third, and her stable didn't meet with much success for the remainder of the season.

TABOOK
6f Handicap   **£1,500-300**   **SP 5-1**

Not the sort of race I usually play, but this horse was outstanding on looks in the paddock and had impressed me when winning on the Rowley Mile in May. The price was two points higher than I'd expected, which confirmed the decision to bet. The value arose from support for Darren Boy which I attributed to hype by John McCririck on the C4 screens which are everywhere at Newmarket. I was wrong and the hype was right, but with only two necks in it at the finish, the bet looks sound.

BALLERINA
7f Handicap £3,800-380 SP 9-1

I had twice seen this well bred and good looking filly running in ten-furlong Listed races at Newbury. On both occasions I felt she had failed to stay. The drop in trip and class seemed likely to suit, making her worth an interest at 10-1. She ran ninth of ten, confirming that she simply hadn't trained on from two to three.

Wednesday July 6   Newmarket

FALLOW
6f 2-y-o Pattern £2,000-320 SP 11-2

My reading of the form for this race made the short-priced pair Knight Commander and Nufooth poor value, as neither had won anything more than ordinary maiden races. I'd identified Fallow and Munguy as the possible value alternatives, but neither took the eye in the paddock. However, on the way to post, Fallow showed a smooth flowing action ideally suited to the fast ground and promised the power that I always seek. If I'm lucky I might see something as clear-cut as this four or five times each year. The offer of 6-1 was snapped up and victory was achieved with some ease.

I saw Fallow several times later in the season and he never again impressed on the way to post as he had at Newmarket, though he invariably started at shorter prices against better opposition. For whatever reason, on July 6, he was at his peak and it showed both before and during the race.

Thursday July 7   Newmarket

SUMMIT
15f Listed £1,000-400 SP 5-2

A three-horse race on my analysis and on the betting. I had seen

Daronne win on firm at Salisbury and felt that he won despite disliking the ground, rather than because firm suited him. I felt that Red Route had been flattered at Ascot because he had been drawn 18 out of 20 over 12 furlongs - he was also unproven at this trip. Summit had run a close third over two miles at Ascot in a better class race and looked standout value to me against public fancies trained by Cecil and Cumani.

This was another case of a horse showing its true ability for the first time in public, as Red Route improved dramatically to win easily and went on to start favourite for the St Leger.

DIABAIG
1m Handicap   **£3,000-300**   **SP 9-1**

From a short list of three, I eliminated Winter Coat on grounds of value (7-2 favourite) and Porphyrios on his appearance in the paddock and his dreadful action going to post. This left Diabaig, a potentially improving filly who looked well. The only thing I got right here was the price, with the winner Paonic also returned at 9-1!

BARATHEA
6f Pattern   **£1,400-400**   **SP 7-2**
Ante-post £3,500-500
Early price £2,000-500

From the first time I saw Barathea in the flesh I thought he looked more like a sprinter than a miler. When he was announced a runner in the July Cup, I saw the opportunity for a value bet with good old public prejudice likely to ensure a stupidly short price for Lochsong. I took the antepost 7-1 and topped up on the day once he was confirmed as a runner and Kinane was booked to ride.

I had expected him to be held up and to be the last horse to challenge, so Kinane's tactics were a surprise. But I gave up blaming jockeys for losing bets some time ago. It is up to the punter to envisage what might happen, and if you get it wrong there is only one person who should be criticised. I remain happy with the value this bet offered and with my staking. If the race were run again, I'd make the same bet.

Another losing Festival meeting, but a substantial win on Duplicity at Newcastle, at early price 16-1, had covered Ascot and Newmarket losses. This was a bet based entirely on the excellent record of high drawn runners in the six-furlong handicap on Northumberland Plate day.

Tuesday July 26   Goodwood

FORTHWITH
10f Handicap   **£6,000-300**   **SP 16-1**

My sort of race, and an opposable favourite in Knowth, who had been very favourably drawn when winning off a 9lb lower mark at Sandown. Forthwith had been running over 12 furlongs, but her best form was at ten furlongs last season. She looked very well, and the stable was showing better form after a duff run in June and had won with Broadway Flyer earlier in the afternoon.

We'll never know if I was right or wrong as Forthwith pulled up injured and is unlikely to reappear.

SOVINISTA
7f Listed   **£4,000-200**   **SP 16-1**

A small wager on a live outsider, well drawn in another race with a poor favourite - Marina Park, rated unlucky last time but not by me - and a couple of doubtful stayers prominent in the betting. She simply wasn't good enough, and one of the non-stayers made all.

Readers will note that the stake here, as on some other occasions, is below the minimum amount quoted in Chapter Thirteen on Money. This reflects the fact that for a bet like this, a potential return of £4,000 is more than adequate. Pushing the stake up to £250 would only reflect slavish adherence to rules, rather than a commonsense approach to the value of a specific bet.

LENNOX LEWIS
6f Nursery   **£2,500-350**   **SP 7-1**

Not usually the sort of race I'd get involved in, but I'd been impressed by this horse when he won from stall ten at Ripon, beating a useful rival who had obtained the favoured stands rail early in the race, with the pair four lengths clear of the third.

The presence of Dettori on board suggested he (or his agent) also thought that was good form. In the parade he looked a typical sprinter, compact, well muscled with powerful quarters, and he moved very well to post, which decided me to bet. He won tidily, always looking able to go on from three out.

Wednesday July 27   Goodwood

PROVENCE

2½m Handicap   £3,000-300   SP 10-1

I'd been waiting for Provence to run over farther than two miles ever since I'd seen him finish third behind Admirals Well over two miles at Kempton in May. His previous record showed wins over two and a quarter miles and very few horses truly stay this sort of trip. The stable had been in good form all season. A big disappointment as he dropped out tamely in the straight and his trainer is now talking about retirement - for the horse, that is.

RAMBRINO

7f 2-y-o Pattern   £1,800-400   SP 9-2

I was unconvinced by the hype for the Cecil-trained favourite Eltish, and Rambrino looked by far the most likely to benefit if he wasn't up to the task. This bet fits one of my preferred scenarios - the longer priced horse in a perceived two-horse race, where the other is a short-priced favourite. But it proved a duff bet this time, and the hype proved well founded.

ALCOVE

1½m Handicap   £3,300-300   SP 11-1

The favourite, Midnight Legend, had won from the best possible draw at Ascot and looked over-rated to me, and the 'steamer' from early 10-1 to 11-2, Mystic Hill, failed to impress in the paddock, being a small light-framed horse with little scope for improvement.

From a short list of three (Alcove, Lombardic, Brandon Court), I opted for the good looking Alcove, who moved down best of the three and looked likely to get the strong pace that seemed to suit him. He got the pace all right - Piggott set off in front so fast that I knew my fate after two furlongs, and the favourite looks better than I rated him.

Thursday July 28   Goodwood

TIOMAN ISLAND

2m Pattern   **£3,300-300**   **SP 10-1**

Tioman Island topped my short list over Summit and Witness Box. He'd run an excellent race from a handicap mark of 105 in the Northumberland Plate, and in my book any horse who runs well off 100+ in a top handicap is good business in Listed or Group 3 company as they are generally underrated thanks to 'Public Prejudice'. The well-backed favourite here was My Patriarch, a horse who had run away in the Ascot Gold Cup, and whose overall form on fast ground was about a stone behind Tioman Island.

I'd expected only around 7-1 to be offered for Tioman Island, which I rated too little in a competitive 15-runner race, but offers of 11-1 found in the ring provided a good value bet for a certain stayer proven on the ground. The moral is: always check prices in the ring, even if you think they won't be what you hope.

CRAGGANMORE

1m Handicap   **£5,400-200**   **SP 20-1**

This was a high drawn horse who had been raised 3lb by the official handicapper for his latest run, but was running off his old mark here, and yet was offered at 25-1 and in one place at 33-1. The favourite, Jawaal, was theoretically 14lb better in here than his current mark, but being drawn eight of 19 gave him an impossible task in my book and his SP of 2-1 puts him high on the list of 'dreadful favourites of the year'. He produced a brilliant performance in defeat, just touched off by two high drawn horses Fraam (15) and Face North (12). My bet finished sixth, and I've no complaints at that. His subsequent win over seven furlongs in Listed company at York suggests that is his best trip, but confirms that he was excellent value here.

HESELL STREET

7f Handicap	£3,000-210	SP 12-1
	£100 Tote Win	

Another race that needed a high drawn horse to provide a value bet, and another poorly drawn favourite in Indian Fly (9). The bet was the best looker and mover from the short list, indeed one of the best movers seen on the fast ground during the entire meeting. She didn't have much luck in running, but the real problem was being too far off the pace on the home turn, and fourth was a fair performance. The winner was drawn 16 and wasn't even on my long list!

Friday July 29   Goodwood

LATTAM

10f Handicap	£3,000-360	SP 15-2

This was a one-horse short list after form study, as ignoring his run as 'pacemaker' in the Eclipse, I felt he had run an excellent race at Ascot over 12 furlongs from a low draw behind Midnight Legend, and would be suited by the drop back to ten furlongs. I assessed his price at around 5-1, so that getting 8-1 was good value. His stable also had an excellent record in this race.

He ran poorly, setting the pace, which I hadn't expected, and was soon beaten in the straight. His pacemaking work may have spoiled him.

DUKE OF EUROLINK

12f Rated Stakes	£2,450-700	SP 7-2

Form study had reduced this race to a clear cut two-horse contest between the bet and Glide Path. The others were either too high in the handicap or running over the wrong trip and/or on the wrong ground. Duke of Eurolink had run very well in the Magnet Cup at York from a poor draw, looked superb in the paddock, and moved to post in a fashion that more than justified the high stake. It might have been more if I'd had more time!

He won with a surge of power at the finish, despite Eddery managing to find more blockages than a Dyno-rod man on overtime.

Over the four days at Goodwood, I found just three winners from 14 bets, but logged a profit of £5,880. This shows how the strategy of seeking value longshots and limiting the bets at shorter odds to those when confidence is high, can produce excellent returns.

Over those same four days, ten horses started favourite at odds of 2-1 or less, and five of them won. But £500 level-stake bets on those ten horses would have produced a profit of less than £400. Life is much harder for favourite backers.

Tuesday August 16   York

ALWAYS ALOOF
14f Rated Stakes   **£1,600-400**   **SP 4-1**

In a small field with four running from out of the handicap, and stamina and temperament doubts about several runners, I made Always Aloof a stand-out bet on form. Proven at the trip and on fast ground, he was the pick of the paddock. A good bet to start the Ebor meeting with a winner.

In assessing this race I ignored my own observations about the effect of the draw at York, assuming that in a nine-runner field it wouldn't affect the result. In the event the first four home came from stalls one to four, with an eight-length gap back to the fifth horse home. A mistake, but not one I would repeat during the remainder of the meeting.

CUFF LINK
2m Listed   **£5,000-370**   **SP 12-1**

One of the best value bets of the year. I awaited this race all day with a sense of anticipation, a tingle that I associate with past big wins on long priced horses. I simply knew that Cuff Link would run a big race, even if he didn't win. My overnight analysis had identified flaws with each of his seven opponents. The first and second in the betting were three-year-olds, but that age group has a very poor record in this race. Third favourite Shareek was a professional loser. My Patriarch had been hyped at Ascot and Goodwood and disappointed in both races, in my view because of the fast ground. Further Flight had won this before, but had shown no sign of that form this season. Oh So Risky would be held up, probably in last, and that style doesn't work often at York. Key To My Heart was unlikely to stay two miles.

Cuff Link, a two-and-three-quarter-mile winner at Ascot, had guaranteed stamina, had shown me power when winning earlier at Salisbury over 14 furlongs, had run well off a high mark in the Northumberland Plate in which Tioman Island had finished third and acted on fast ground. He looked fit and moved easily to post - time to go to work.

In the ring I made three bets of £1,000-70 and one of £2,000-160 after the 14-1 dried up. A better example of betting 'Against The Crowd' would be hard to find.

In a tight finish, from my position 150 yards from the line, I thought that My Patriarch had just held on, but the photo result was called in my favour. A stewards' inquiry had been announced, but like most punters (and bookmakers), I assumed this concerned My Patriarch bumping Further Flight when he pushed his way into the lead two furlongs out. When the announcement of an amended result came some ten minutes later, I was stunned.

In his excellent book The Winning Horseplayer, *the American professional Andy Beyer tells how, after similar set-backs, he has learned to 'accept tough losses with bemused detachment'. I hope that I can acquire that skill in future years, but I haven't got there yet. Beyer also reports that earlier in his career, his analysis and betting would suffer when he was outraged by what he perceived as injustice. He lost thousands of dollars as a result.*

I took this part of his writing to heart, and after a restless night, concluded I was in no state to go to work again on the Wednesday. Instead I drove home and watched the coverage on C4, without having a bet. My opinion of the York stewards remains unprintable, but at least I didn't take it out on my wallet.

Thursday August 18   York

Having studied the handicaps on Wednesday evening, with analysis concentrated on the low drawn runners, I felt ready to have a couple of off-course bets on Thursday. I was confident that my understanding of the draw bias would more than compensate for the off-course tax.

LAP OF LUXURY

1m Handicap   £2,500-250 Tax Paid SP 10-1

With two of the four low drawn horses, Watani and Paonic, likely to contest a strong pace, I favoured Lap Of Luxury to sit in behind and benefit from the tow. The race worked out almost exactly as expected, with Lap Of Luxury heading Paonic inside the final 100 yards.

The first three home were drawn four, three and two and finished seven lengths clear of the fourth. Whilst pleased with the win (which illogically felt like revenge on the stewards), after the race my head started swimming with what I could have earned from possible forecast and tricast combinations. If punters were limited to a two-word vocabulary, the two words would surely be: 'If Only.'

FOUNDRY LANE

1½m Handicap   £2,500-250 Tax Paid   SP 11-1

From stall one, Foundry Lane's form looked much better than those drawn two, four and five, with stall three a non-runner. Assuming everybody else would by now be able to see what I had seen, I took the early price 10-1. Remarkably, despite the evidence of the results at the meeting to date, Laxford Bridge went off 5-1 favourite despite being drawn 13. Foundry Lane was outpaced three out, but kept to the favoured inside he progressed into second at the line even though he appeared to be struggling all the way. The winner came from stall seven and returned 16-1.

So I managed a profit on the three days. But the loss of the return on Cuff Link inevitably had a considerable effect on my profit margin for the year, especially when added to the loss of a further four thousand after the (justified) disqualification of Avro Anson at Cheltenham. I look forward to the day when fate evens up the score and some kindly bunch of stewards throw an undeserved few grand in my direction.

For those who feel that my harping on about the draw at York is overdone, and that the draw can't have that much influence, try looking at the results for the very next day's meeting at Chester. The first four races were all won by the horse drawn one, respectively at 9-4 by five lengths, 7-2 by five lengths, 7-2 by seven lengths and 5-1 by six lengths. The fifth race was over two miles but still ended with stall three beating stall two, and the final race saw stall three at 10-1 beat stall one at 7-1.

Wednesday September 7   Doncaster

NEW REPUTATION

14f Handicap	£3,000-210	SP 14-1
	£50 Tote Win	

This was a bet on a horse I had opted to follow after his run at Newbury last time, when he had shown me the power despite finishing only fifth in a qualifier for this final. At Newbury he led three furlongs out until headed by the winner at the one-furlong pole and was then eased once beaten. I was confident that the longer trip would suit him and had noted an entry for the Cesarewitch.

His performance here got good reviews from the formbooks and press, which led to him starting as short as 9-1 later at Newmarket, but it didn't please me much. He was soon in last place in a field of 17 and his fast-finishing seventh place owed much to others easing down once the winner had gone clear. I probably chose the right horse, but the wrong day.

The £50 Tote bet reflects the small size of the Tote pools at this meeting.

ELFIN LAUGHTER

1m Nursery	£2,000-400	SP 5-1

In seven-furlong and mile nursery handicaps I like to back horses who have already won a nursery at the trip. These races often contain well backed horses who are maidens, or whose form is all at shorter trips. Most punters are suckers for the 'fast finisher' over six furlongs when he moves up in distance and these horses ensure the value. The previous winner has proven stamina and has shown that he is fairly handicapped.

Elfin Laughter had won by two and a half lengths over a mile at Ayr, but faded to finish 14th of 16 here, one of the first to point to the slump that Hannon's horses suffered during September.

Thursday September 8   Doncaster

POPPY CAREW

1m 2-y-o Pattern   **£1,600-400**   **SP 7-2**

I had backed Poppy Carew at 16-1 when she finished second in a seven-furlong Group 3 race at Goodwood last time. Her performance there warranted a follow up bet in what looked, at best, a race of equal merit. From the in-form yard of Peter Harris, her form would have produced a much shorter price if she had had a more fashionable trainer.

Third place behind a couple of well-bred maiden race winners was slightly disappointing, but the sort of result that is all in a day's work.

ARCADIAN HEIGHTS

2¼m Pattern   **£1,500-400**   **SP 7-2**

Upped in class and looking nothing like so well as he had at York, I deserted Cuff Link (no value at 9-2 anyway), in favour of the proven class and stamina of Arcadian Heights. Despite a dodgy reputation, he had done nothing wrong this season and looked a fair 2-1 chance in my eyes. He made all with Dettori showing fine pace judgement, which is without doubt the quality that separates him from most of his fellow jockeys.

NONIOS

7f Handicap   **£2,750-250**   **SP 11-1**

By this stage of the meeting, it was clear that low numbers had an edge in races on the straight course, at least in big fields. I opted for Nonios, drawn four, to provide some value against the heavily backed favourite Polish Admiral, drawn seven.

The favourite won easily, with Nonios in fourth and never looking likely to trouble the winner. The first four home were drawn seven, two, six and four.

SONIC BOY

7f Conditions £700-400 SP 13-8

A bet at below my normal minimum price, brought about by seeing Sonic Boy in the paddock and moving to post. He would feature in the top five good looking horses during the entire season, and went down at least as well as Fallow and Duke of Eurolink. Well clear on my form analysis and on Timeform ratings, he drifted in the betting from 11-10. I could see no reason for this and stepped in when he reached 7-4, confident of boosting my profit on the day.

He was beaten by Hannon's only winner of the week and so far as I could see, he had no excuse.

Friday September 9   Doncaster

CAPIAS

1½m Listed £1,800-400 SP 9-2

I had seen this good looking, lightly-raced horse win a ten-furlong maiden at the Newmarket July meeting, and again when he was outclassed in the Voltigeur Stakes at York. This looked the right level of competition and he appealed as a horse to follow.

In the end he disappointed by finishing fifth, but still ran pretty well as he was beaten only just over a length. He'll be an interesting horse as a four-year-old if he remains in this country. The winner, Estimraar, went off at 25-1. After that sort of result I always go back to the formbook to see whether I could have made a case for the winner, because 9-2 winners are my bread and butter, but 25-1 shots provide the jam. And whilst he wasn't obvious short list material, neither was he a genuine 25-1 chance on his record in a race with no stand-out favourite.

OPTIONS OPEN

7f 2-y-o Pattern £1,800-400 SP 9-2

A big mistake. I wanted to bet on this race, because I felt that Alami was a false favourite on the basis of two easy wins in minor company over six furlongs at Pontefract. I had seen Options Open win the Acomb Stakes at York when he showed the power, going clear two furlongs out and then holding on close home. By now I was aware that Hannon was struggling, but I was fooled by the win of Prussian Flag over Sonic Boy, and decided that the worst was over. The only other runner to start at less than 10-1 was the eventual winner Sri Pekan, who touched 9-2 before going off at 100-30.

It took only a few minutes' hindsight to realise that I'd chosen the wrong one of the two, regardless of the result. Sri Pekan had solid Pattern race form, came from a stable in reasonable form and was quite simply the better value bet when both were on offer at 9-2. My expectation had been that Sri Pekan would start at around 9-4, maybe touching 5-2. I didn't have the flexibility to switch when I saw the market - a lesson learnt, one hopes.

SHADOWS OF SILVER
1½m Handicap   £5,000-330   SP 14-1

In an open race a 'Kitchi Koo' bet on a 16-1 shot who had winning form, came from a good stable and had an inside draw in a big field. I thought some of the more fancied horses would struggle from a low (outside) draw.

Shadows of Silver was one of a group of high drawn horses who went off too fast, taking each other on. She faded in the straight, and the first four home all came from well off the pace. They had started from stalls three, four, five and two.

Sometimes you just get a race hopelessly wrong and the only thing to do is shrug it off and try to think about something else during the long haul back down the M1.

Shadows of Silver won her next two races, both at Redcar over one and three-quarter miles, at odds of 11-1 and 100-30. And the answer is: 'No, I didn't'.

Friday November 11   Cheltenham

DEAR DO
2½m H'cap Hurdle   £6,000-340   SP 16-1

A classic example of the 'Kitchi Koo' principle. I had seen this horse on SIS running a fair race over two and a quarter miles on his seasonal debut for the same claiming rider and rated him value here in a race that contained several runners from out of form stables. A slowly-run race became a sprint from three out and he wasn't well placed when the sprint started. I had anticipated that Dagaz would front run, but he unseated at the first hurdle!

Nothing else appealed on a day of small fields and short-priced favourites.

Saturday November 12   Cheltenham

DAKYNS BOY

3½ H'cap Chase	£1,200-400	SP 3-1

Dakyns Boy was on my list of horses to follow for the season and this race looked ideal for him if he was fit. He looked well in the paddock, whereas the favourite Antonin looked even smaller and leaner than he had last season. In a small field the price looked good value.

But for a blunder at the last, he might have won, but no complaints. There will be other occasions during a jump season when I benefit from a mistake at the last by opponents.

EGYPT MILL PRINCE

2½m H'cap Chase	Ante-post £3,000-250
	Early price£2,500-250

The Mackeson is one of a number of major jumping races that are susceptible to analysis by investigation of past results, which show that most winners fit a particular pattern. I look at age, weight, previous course form, odds and trainer. Looking at the last 15 runnings of this race we find:

- 12 winners were eight years old or younger
- No winner carried ten stones or was out of the handicap
- Ten were in the price range 5-1 to 8-1 and none was over 12-1
- Eight had previous win or placed form in top class races at Cheltenham
- The last ten winners were trained in leading southern stables.

My selection was the only probable runner to fit all five requirements if my guess at his likely SP was correct. I took 12-1 from my local Ladbrokes (my only visit of the entire year) on Wednesday, and the early price 10-1 from Tote Credit.

Egypt Mill Prince didn't jump as well as he had on previous visits and seemed unhappy when taken on at halfway by Tipping Tim. The winner Bradbury Star fitted all the criteria listed above, except for being a nine-year-old.

JUDGES FANCY
3¼m H'cap Hurdle   £200 Tote Win

A Tote value bet on a plodder likely to appreciate the softening ground on a rainy day. The Tote price just before the off was 12-1 compared with the S.P. of 13-2. He plodded slowly into fourth place, beaten seven and a half lengths, looking as if another circuit would have suited him.

MARTINS LAMP
2m Novice Chase   £2,200-800   SP 5-2

Martins Lamp was high on my list of horses to follow. I had seen all three of his runs at Towcester two seasons earlier as a novice hurdler and been deeply impressed by his looks and his performances. This looked a great value bet because I was certain that Absaloms Lady wouldn't be suited by the left-handed track, and that she was over-rated on the basis of her second to Travado at Exeter. Martins Lamp looked very fit in the paddock and with the Nicholson stable in good form, I bet with confidence.

The result was never in doubt, with the favourite losing ground by jumping away to her right. Another prime example of the value to be obtained by opposing dubious odds-on favourites with a solid second or third choice in the betting.

Friday November 25   Newbury

Three years to the day since my redundancy, and I went to Newbury with friends who had suffered the same fate. Having partaken of alcohol beforehand, I limited my involvement to watching until the last race.

STRONG GROVE
2¹/₂m Novice Hurdle   **£600-300**   **SP 15-8**

I had seen this mare win at Wincanton on her debut, beating the useful Going Around who had a Grade 2 success on his record. Her only opposition here seemed to be from the Bailey-trained Feel The Power, who was making his seasonal debut. I had expected that Strong Grove would start a shade of odds-on, so offers of 2-1 compelled a bet. This time the hype merchants were right and Feel The Power won in a canter.

Saturday November 26   Newbury

A high-class card, but small fields and short priced favourites limited the betting opportunities.

THE FROG PRINCE
2¹/₂m Novice Chase   **£1,000-500**   **SP 7-4**

This horse had run really well over course and distance when looking patently unfit on his seasonal debut. With his stable now in better form, and The Frog Prince looking transformed in the paddock, this was a must bet. The main betting opposition came from the Nicholson yard, in the form of the Irish point-to-point winner Approach The Stars. These Irish winners are often hyped as future stars, but the standards in Irish pointing are abysmal and opposing these horses will always pay in the long run, especially on their debut over English fences.

Summary

With no bets placed on the middle day at York, the diary represents a pretty typical picture from 23 betting days. A total of 63 bets produced eleven winners. Turnover of £25,400 produced a profit of £2,525.

Almost any representative sample of my betting over the past five years would produce the same sort of winner/runner ratio and the same sort of minimum percentage profit on turnover.

It is the purple patches, some of which were mentioned earlier in the book, that push profits higher, but the key to making a living wage remains the ability to produce a steady profit level year in, year out.

There were good days and bad days, good meetings and bad meetings, but throughout the pattern remains the same. More losers than winners, more losing days than winning days, and so on. In his book *Betting For A Living*, buried in the chapter titled 'How To Bet', Nick Mordin offers a sentence that perfectly describes this process:

'To become a winner, you must accept losing on a scale you would presently find unacceptable.'

Or, to put it another way, making decent profits requires adequate starting capital.

The bets recorded in the diary should demonstrate clearly why confidence and capital are necessary, to cope with losses such as those sustained at the Cheltenham Festival.

Chapter Fifteen

Happy endings

The business of being a full-time professional punter is very much the same as setting up a small business in any other field of endeavour. I am using my capital to invest in backing my judgement of the market, employing the expertise and experience gained from 30 years of punting and racegoing. And it bears repeating that, as with any other business, inadequate capital is the likeliest cause of failure.

But of course I have several advantages over the average self-employed person. I don't have to deal with the Inland Revenue or the Vatman, since gambling winnings are tax free. I don't need premises, or the services of solicitors, accountants or any of the other leeches of the professional world. I don't have to spend much of my time issuing invoices and chasing up bad debts, since course bookmakers pay on the dot or go out of business very quickly.

However, these are as nothing compared to the gains over my previous life as a nine-to-five office bound slave. No commuting, no managers to be placated, no office politics, no fear of redundancy, no schedules, no deadlines, no middle of the night telephone calls. I have achieved the ambition of so many, by turning my hobby into my job.

I started betting, fascinated by the challenge of solving the puzzle that a horse race represented, and the challenge remains a driving force to this day. Starting work on the form study for a race is not unlike starting a crossword puzzle - all the clues are there and the correct solution can be found. But solving a horse race offers the chance of financial gain far above that on offer for completing a crossword!

There is a school of thought amongst Freudians (Clement excepted), that gambling is simply a displacement for sexual activity. Indeed, anyone who has spent an afternoon in a city centre betting shop may well feel that it's the only form of sexual activity most of the inmates are ever likely to experience. Certainly there is a rhythm to betting, with the foreplay of the paddock inspection, the excitement of placing the bet and the climax of the race itself, which offers much support for such a theory. However, betting does have the advantage, in this politically correct age, that nobody expects you to rush round to the winners' enclosure and ask the horses 'How was it for you'?

Although I have to do a good deal of driving, much of it is through beautiful countryside, with time to explore quiet villages and discover delightful out of the way pubs. Although most serious punters will tell you that alcohol and gambling don't mix, I've always enjoyed a couple of pints at lunchtime as a preliminary to the afternoon, although more than two is very likely to induce unwarranted confidence.

Many racing books are padded out at this stage with lists of racecourses, acres of past results, or other similar material which can be found in plenty of other sources. As a diversion from that sort of waffle I offer my list of favourite pubs, most of which are so hard to find that it will take a host of determined readers to fill them to the point where their virtues will be lost.

Ascot	*The Queen Victoria* in Binfield
Bath	*The White Hart* in Ford
Cheltenham	*The High Roost* on Cleeve Hill
Chepstow	*The Brockweir Inn* in Brockweir
Exeter	*The Ley Arms* in Kenn
Fontwell	*The Labour in Vain* in Eastergate
Goodwood	*The Blacksmiths Arms* in Donnington
Hereford	*The Butchers Arms* in Woolhope
Newbury	*The Axe and Compasses* in East End
Newmarket	*The Kings* (Dyke End) in Reach
Salisbury	*The Ship Inn* in Burcombe
Stratford	*The Blue Boar* in Binton
Taunton	*The Half Moon* in Stoke St Mary
Towcester	*The New Inn* in Abthorpe
Worcester	*The Old Chequers* in Crowle

All of these are quiet village or country pubs offering decent beer, sufficiently far off the beaten track to discourage the coachloads of lager drinkers who throng so many pubs in the vicinity of the racecourse.

And if you spot a quiet, studious punter in the corner, head buried in a racing paper or a pint of bitter, you can take the opportunity to tell the author exactly what you think of the ramblings you had to endure before discovering the only useful bit of information in the entire book.

Appendices

Appendix 1

Longshot bets 1993

Date	Horse	Stake	To Win	Result
7/1	Mighty Randolph	200	3200	L
14/1	Kalzari	210	4000	L
16/1	Uncle Eli	190	3000	L
22/1	Miss Fern	250	2500	L
26/1	Fremantle	90	3000	L
30/1	Latent Talent	250	5000	L
4/2	Radical Request	220	3000	L
6/2	Lake Tereen	300	5000	L
6/2	Peanuts Pet	310	5000	L
13/2	Emerald Sunset	300	6000	L
15/2	Auction Law	240	3000	L
25/2	Mr Jamboree	280	3000	L
16/3	Boraceva	300	3000	L
16/3	Cairncastle	400	5000	L
17/3	Superior Finish	320	4000	L
17/3	Bishops Island	500	7500	L
18/3	The Red One	400	4000	L
18/3	Diamond Cut	300	4500	L
20/3	Willsford	300	3600	L
27/3	Kiwi Velocity	400	5000	L
1/4	Peaceman	260	5000	L
10/4	Blue Dart	250	3500	L
13/4	Carrick Lanes	300	3000	L
18/5	Remany	300	3000	L
22/5	Press Gallery	260	3000	L
26/5	Turgenev	300	3100	L
29/5	El Cortes	220	4000	L

Longshot bets 1993 *(cont.)*

Date	Horse	Stake	To Win	Result
12/6	Heavenly Risk	250	2500	L
15/6	Balasani	500	6000	W
16/6	King Athelstan	200	4000	L
26/6	Jura Forest	400	4000	W
26/6	True Precision	200	2400	L
16/7	Humam	300	3000	L
24/7	Jade Vale	300	3300	L
27/7	Allwight Then	250	3500	L
7/8	Yours By Right	460	9000	L
2/9	Lacerta	240	3000	L
9/9	Jack Button	200	2000	L
18/9	Western Cape	420	5100	L
18/9	Walking The Plank	300	6000	L
6/11	Avro Anson	420	4600	L
12/11	Light Veneer	530	6600	W
17/11	Woodlands Genhire	200	3000	L
29/11	Uluru	320	3500	W
3/12	Kings Treasure	270	3000	L
3/12	Annio Chilone	500	6800	L
9/12	Staunch Rival	250	3000	W
18/12	Windy Ways	320	6000	L

Appendix 2

30 major Flat handicaps, all of which should be studied with a view to a bet.

April	Spring Cup	Newbury	Low draw
	Esher Cup	Sandown	
May	Chester Cup	Chester	
	Whitsun Cup	Sandown	
June	Ascot Stakes	Ascot	
	Royal Hunt Cup	Ascot	
	Bessborough H'cap	Ascot	High draw exc on soft
	King George V	Ascot	Ditto
	Britannia H'cap	Ascot	
	Northumberland Plate	Newcastle	Ignore Ascot runners
July	Hong Kong Trophy	Sandown	High numbers best
	Old Newton Cup	Haydock	
	Duke of Cambridge	Newmarket	
	Magnet Cup	York	
	Goodwood Stakes	Goodwood	
	Tote Gold Trophy	Goodwood	
	Golden Mile	Goodwood	Ignore stalls 1-12
	Spitfire H'cap	Goodwood	
August	Melrose Stakes	York	Ignore stalls 10+
	Tote Ebor	York	Ditto
	Bradford & Bingley H'cap	York	Low draw
Sept	Harcros Timber H'cap	Doncaster	
	Coalite Rated Stakes	Doncaster	
	Courage Stakes	Newbury	
	Autumn Cup	Newbury	
	Rothmans North South Final	Newbury	
	Festival H'cap	Ascot	
October	Cambridgeshire H'cap	Newmarket	
	Cesarewitch H'cap	Newmarket	

Appendix 3

NH Horses to Follow 1994/5

ALL FOR LUCK   M Pipe   2^1/$_2$-3 Hcp Chases

Produced four consecutive wins in the spring, two at Newbury and one at Aintree, before failing in a classy novice handicap at Punchestown. He seemed unhappy with the fences there and looks unsuited to a right-handed track - he was well beaten at Taunton also early in the season. On decent ground, going left-handed, he looks capable of further improvement and could well feature in the Mackeson Gold Cup.

ARCTIC COURSE   D Nicholson   2^1/$_2$-3m Nov Chases

A big strong, good looking chestnut with point to point form in Ireland, he lacked the pace to trouble the best over hurdles last season, but won twice at Worcester and was narrowly beaten at Chepstow in novice hurdles. Looks certain to go chasing this season and likely to prove better over fences. Has already proved he stays three miles and acts on good and soft ground.

BASS ROCK   I Balding   2^1/$_2$m Hcp Hurdles/ Nov Chases

I rate this as the best looking horse I saw running in novice hurdles last season. He started last year in bumpers, then won a two and a quarter mile novice hurdle at Exeter on soft ground, before falling when odds-on on firm ground at the same track. Certain to start the year on a fair handicap mark, he could win handicap hurdles, or he could be switched to novice chasing. Either way he should win more races.

BRIEF GALE   J Gifford   2m-3m Nov Chases

Far and away the best mare running in novice hurdles last season, she has a touch of class. If she takes to jumping fences, then she will dominate in mares' novice chases and could take on the males successfully as well.

CAPTAIN DOLFORD   D Gandolfo   3m+ Hcp Hurdles

No surprise to those who know me and went to Cheltenham last March, when this horse disappointed in the long distance handicap hurdle. His previous two wins on heavy ground at Newbury and Chepstow had marked him as an improving stayer, and I expect him to develop again this season given the soft ground he obviously needs. He isn't very big and I'd be surprised if he was switched to novice chases, where I doubt if he'd be successful.

CHIEFS SONG   S Dow   2^1/$_4$-2^3/$_4$m Hcp Hurdles

Well clear at Fontwell last December when the commentator announced he 'only had to jump the last to win'. Thanks to that intervention he remains a novice and should be able to use his experience to good effect this season and could move on to handicaps in which his trainer has an excellent record of producing horses to a series of wins.

COLLIER BAY   J Old   2¹/4-2³/4 Hcp Hurdles

A big leggy sort who moved to Jim Old from John Gosden, who trained him on the Flat. Won two small novice hurdles on heavy ground, the first by 20l and the second by a distance. Withdrawn from the Triumph Hurdle on the day of the race, presumably due to the fast ground, a move which won't have harmed his handicap mark. Potentially top class and might finally stop Jim Old from going on and on about Mole Board!

DAKYNS BOY   N Twiston-Davies 3m+ Hcp Chases

A useful novice two seasons ago, he only ran three times last season and didn't reappear after finishing third in a three and a half mile chase on Mackeson Gold Cup day. Still young enough to show improvement if he can be returned fully fit and could develop into a National horse eventually. The only question mark in my mind is that he might be best suited by a right hand track, which would rule out Cheltenham, and the Welsh, Scottish, Midland and Aintree Grand Nationals! Unsuited by firm ground.

DOMINIE   J Edwards   2-2¹/2m Nov Hurdles

Won a bumper at Kempton by 20l despite only taking the lead 300 yards from the finish and later ran respectably in the championship bumper races at Cheltenham and Punchestown. If he takes to hurdling he has the potential to go to the top.

GENERAL WOLFE T Forster   2¹/2-3m Nov Chases

Very unusually for a Tim Forster-trained horse, he won a two-mile, five-furlong novice hurdle at Towcester as a four-year-old last autumn. A grand looking horse who is certain to be given plenty of time and started off in minor company, he should win novice chases at the minor tracks. But ignore him if he is kept to hurdles as he looks likely to lack the speed for that game.

GLENTOWER   N Henderson 2¹/2m Nov Chases

A smashing looking horse who won a two-mile, five-furlong novice handicap over hurdles at Newbury in March on his fourth outing and was then put away to await this season. Potentially a top class chaser and in a stable that has had plenty of experience with this sort of horse.

GROUND NUT   H Knight   2¹/2m Hcp Hurdles

Won a decent juvenile hurdle at Wincanton, but was well beaten next time in the Triumph Hurdle, which should ensure he starts this season on a good handicap mark. He looks likely to stay farther than two miles and should be able to win in handicap company.

JOHNNY KELLY J J O'Neill   2¹/2-3m Nov Chases

The obligatory northern-trained contender to follow up the successes of Beachy Head last year. This ex-Irish horse won easily at Kelso and then ran really well against more experienced rivals at Aintree, a race he looked likely to win three from home. Certain to win novice chases in the north, he could be good enough to raid southern tracks as well.

MAILCOM   J Pitman   3m+ Hcp Chases

Had a fair season as a novice, but disappointed at Cheltenham even allowing for the fact that he was hampered during the three-mile novice chase at the Festival. In the right stable to go on improving in handicap company and will be suited by long distances, good or soft going and a left hand track - the sort to win around Warwick and Uttoxeter before taking the three and a quarter mile handicap at Newbury just after Xmas.

MARTINS LAMP   J Gifford   2m Nov Chases
Exceptionally good looking and useful novice hurdler two years ago, winning twice at Towcester. Missed all last season and carried forward from last year's list in the hope that he'll be brought back fit and well. A horse of considerable potential.

MR JERVIS   J Gifford   2¹/2m Nov Hurdles
Looked to be improving rapidly at the end of last season, when he finished up running third in the EBF Nov Final at Cheltenham in April from 8lb out of the handicap. Still only five-year-old, so likely to be kept to hurdling this season and his experience should ensure success in novice company.

RIVER MANDATE T Forster   2¹/2m-3m Hcp Chases
A grand looking horse who runs in the Arkle colours. He ended last season by winning the same Towcester two and three-quarter mile novice chase that went to Cherrykino two years earlier, having won over two and a half miles at Ludlow earlier in the year. Took a while to get his jumping together, but highly likely to improve through the season and prove useful around the second division tracks.

RIVER ISLAND   J Old   2m Hcp Hurdles
On the list last year, when he ran only once and finished almost last at Windsor. Still only a five-year-old and if he is back to full fitness he could have a useful season in handicap hurdles. As a novice he seemed to prefer soft ground and a right-handed track.

SHAAB TURBO   S Cole   2¹/2m Nov/Hcp Chases
From the same stable as Dubacilla and Just So, he showed good form in novice company last season until well beaten in a valuable novice handicap at Ascot on his last run. That defeat should ensure he remains on a good handicap mark, and his trainer has already shown that he can handle a decent horse on its rise through the ranks. Likely to score at the West Country tracks.

SMITHS BAND   J Pitman   3m Nov Chases
Disappointing over hurdles last season after a debut second to Arctic Course at Worcester over two miles, five furlongs on heavy ground. Likely to do much better over fences and his modest form should ensure decent prices when he starts off in novice chases.

TARAMOSS   J Edwards   3m+ Hcp Chases
A tough stayer who ended last year by winning the Tote Novice Chase Final at Uttoxeter on soft ground. He'll be suited by trips in excess of three miles on soft ground and could develop into a Midland National winner by next March.

THE BRUD   S Sherwood   2-2¹/₂m Nov Hurdles

This year's horse you've never heard of - and may never hear of again! He only ran twice last season and was pulled up lame when odds-on favourite in a four runner race at Ayr on fast ground, having previously run unplaced at Cheltenham in January. He is however a big, good looking horse with plenty of scope for improvement if he returns to action, and he isn't likely to be odds-on again for a while!

TOTHEWOODS   N Twiston-Davies   3m Nov Chases

These days this sort of list has to include at least one novice chaser trained by the Twister, following the exploits of Young Hustler, Earth Summit and others in the past two years. This one showed decent form in novice hurdles, stays three miles, goes on any ground and looks just the sort of horse that suits the trainer.

WELL BRIEFED   R Buckler   2¹/₂m Hcp Chases

We started with a Mackeson Gold Cup possible, and we end with another one. Although a novice he ran mainly in handicap company last season, and won the major prize at Ascot over two and a half miles in April prior to disappointing on fast ground at Ayr. He also ran second to Monsieur Le Cure at Cheltenham in January, admittedly getting a lot of weight. Jumps very well and sure to improve with experience, he has form going left and right handed, on good and soft ground, and on flat and undulating tracks. An admirable racehorse.

Appendix 4

Bibliography

The following is a list of books etc. that have been mentioned in the previous chapters and may be of interest to readers.

Raceform Form Book
(Combined Official Form Book and Notebook)
Raceform Ltd., Compton Newbury, Berkshire RG16 0NL.
Tel: 01635 578080

Racehorses / Chasers & Hurdlers
Timeform Perspective
Timeform Ratings
Timeform Ltd, Timeform House, Halifax HX1 1XE.
Tel: 01422 330540

Racing Post Weekender (weekly paper)
(formerly The Sporting Life Weekender)
Racing Post, 1 Canada Square, Canary Wharf, London E14 5AB.
Tel: 0171 293 2001

SIS Daily Racing Review
SIS Ltd., 17 Corsham Street, London N1 6BR.
Tel: 0171 696 8695 / 0171 696 8676

The Winning Look by Nick Mordin
Value Betting by Mark Coton (**Out of print**)
Betting for a Living by Nick Mordin
Rowton Press Ltd *(formely Aesculus Press)*, PO Box 10, Oswestry, Salop SY11 1RB.
Tel: 01691 679111

The Winning Horseplayer by Andy Beyer
Available from: Gamblers Book Services, 18 Coleswood Road, Harpenden, Herts AL5 1EQ.
Tel: 01582 712244